Rightfully Ours *How Women Won the Vote*

Rightfully Ours

*How Women
Won the Vote*

21 ACTIVITIES

Kerrie Logan Hollihan

CHICAGO
REVIEW
PRESS

Published by Chicago Review Press, Incorporated

814 North Franklin Street

Chicago, Illinois 60610

ISBN 978-1-883052-89-8

Cover and interior design: Monica Baziuk

Front cover photographs: (*full-bleed image*) Jessie Stubbs (*left*) and "General" Rosalie Jones (*right*), who led women's suffrage hikes to Albany, New York, and Washington, DC | Library of Congress LC-B2-2461-14; (*inset, from left to right*) Elizabeth Cady Stanton and her daughter Harriot | Library of Congress LC-USZ62-48965; Women's League officers from Newport, Rhode Island | Library of Congress LC-USZ62-51555; women marching with signs, 1917 | Library of Congress LC-H261-7104; Susan B. Anthony and Elizabeth Cady Stanton | Library of Congress mnwp 159001; Lucy Burns | Library of Congress mnwp 274009

Back cover photographs (*clockwise from top*): Alice Paul with banner | Library of Congress mnwp 160068; Sojourner Truth | Library of Congress LC-USZ62-119343; women marching | Library of Congress LC-USZ62-10845

Interior illustrations: Mark Baziuk

Image on page vi: Women casting ballots, 1917 | LC-USZ62-75334 DLC

Library of Congress Cataloging-in-Publication Data

Hollihan, Kerrie Logan.

    Rightfully ours : how women won the vote, 21 activities / Kerrie Logan Hollihan. — 1st ed.

        p. cm.

    Includes index.

    ISBN 978-1-883052-89-8 (pbk.)

    1. Women—Suffrage—United States—History—Juvenile literature. 2. Women's rights—United States—History—Juvenile literature. 3. Suffragists—United States—History—Juvenile literature. 4. Women—Suffrage—Study and teaching—Activity programs—United States. 5. Women's rights—Study and teaching—Activity programs—United States. I. Title.

    JK1898.H65 2012

    324.6′230973—dc23

                                          2012006044

Printed in the United States of America

5 4 3 2 1

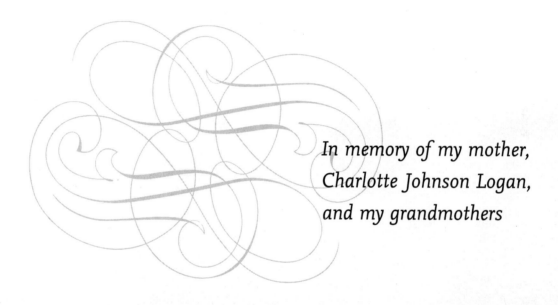

In memory of my mother,
Charlotte Johnson Logan,
and my grandmothers

Contents

A Time Line for Women's Suffrage

July 4, 1776 ➤ The Declaration of Independence is signed in Philadelphia

January 1777 ➤ Mary Katherine Goddard prints the first full copy of the Declaration

1836 ➤ Sarah Grimké speaks publicly against slavery

1837 ➤ Lucretia Mott speaks publicly against slavery

1840 ➤ Elizabeth Cady Stanton and Lucretia Mott are turned away as delegates to the World Anti-Slavery Convention in London

1843 ➤ Lucy Stone enters Oberlin College and is among its first women students

1848 ➤ Elizabeth Cady Stanton, Lucretia Mott, Elizabeth Smith Miller, and two others organize the first women's rights convention in Seneca Falls, New York; Stanton and Elizabeth McClintock write the Declaration of Rights and Sentiments

1849 ➤ Harriet Tubman escapes from slavery and becomes a conductor on the Underground Railroad

1850 ➤ Amelia Bloomer pushes for dress reform by wearing bloomers

1851 ➤ Sojourner Truth makes her "Ain't I a Woman?" speech before a women's rights meeting in Ohio

1852 ➤ Harriet Beecher Stowe publishes *Uncle Tom's Cabin*

1861–1865 ➤ Suffragists set aside their work to aid the North during the Civil War

1868–1871 ➤ The 14th and 15th Amendments to the Constitution give black males citizenship and the vote; women's rights are ignored

1869 ➤ The women's suffrage movement divides over political differences, creating the American Woman Suffrage Association and the National Woman Suffrage Association

1872 ➤ Susan B. Anthony stands trial in Rochester, New York, for trying to vote in the presidential election

1876 ➤ Susan B. Anthony presents a Declaration of Rights for Women at the Centennial Convention in Philadelphia

1878 ➤ Susan B. Anthony writes a women's suffrage amendment to the Constitution

1883 ➤ Frances Willard founds the Woman's Christian Temperance Union

1890 ➤ The suffrage movement reunites to form the National American Woman Suffrage Association

➤ Jane Addams opens Hull House in Chicago and launches the Settlement Movement

1893 ➤ Lucy Stone dies

1895 ➤ Elizabeth Cady Stanton publishes the *Woman's Bible*

1896 ➤ A group of African American women (which includes Harriet Tubman, Mary Church Terrell, and Ida B. Wells-Barnett) found the National Association of Colored Women

1900 ➤ Carrie Chapman Catt and Anna Howard Shaw become leaders of the suffrage movement

1902 ➤ Elizabeth Cady Stanton dies

1906 ➤ Susan B. Anthony dies

1913 ➤ Activists Alice Paul and Lucy Burns leave the National American Woman Suffrage Association to organize the Congressional Union, later the National Woman's Party

1913 ➤ Marchers are attacked as they march in a suffrage parade in Washington, DC

1916 ➤ Jeannette Rankin of Montana becomes the nation's first woman to serve in the US House of Representatives

1917 ➤ The United States enters World War I

1919 ➤ The 19th Amendment passes both the US House of Representatives and the Senate

1920 ➤ Tennessee becomes the 36th state to ratify the 19th Amendment and women's suffrage becomes the law of the land

1923 ➤ Alice Paul writes an Equal Rights Amendment to end discrimination based on gender, which was never ratified

Preface

A Declaration for a New Nation

"We hold these truths to be self-evident, that all men are created equal...."

EARLY IN the new year of 1777, life was tense in revolutionary Baltimore, as it was across the 13 new states. The upstart Americans had launched a revolution against Great Britain and its monarch, King George III. The summer before, Baltimore's citizens had swarmed the streets to hear words of a thrilling document just written in Philadelphia. It declared that "all men were created equal," that they had "certain inalienable rights," and that they were entitled to "life, liberty, and the pursuit of happiness."

There was just one problem. This Declaration of Independence was handwritten on parchment with a quill pen and ink. Any printed copies were incomplete,

★ OPPOSITE: Suffragists staged a tableau at the US Treasury Department steps during their monumental parade in Washington, DC, in 1913.

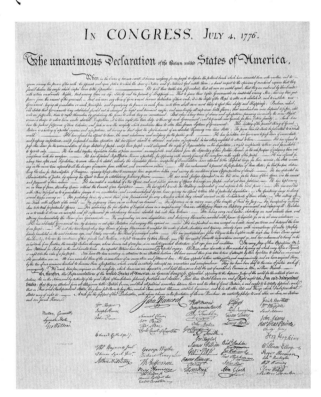

because they didn't show the signatures of those who had penned their names at the bottom of the page.

It was high time to put these radical words—along with the names of the brave men who had signed it—into the hands of people across the colonies. The document needed a publisher to print it in full.

★ **ABOVE:** The Declaration of Independence.

National Archives

★ **LEFT:** Mary Katherine Goddard printed the first full copies of the Declaration of Independence.

Library of Congress bdsdcc 02101

That duty fell to a woman named Mary Katherine Goddard, editor of the *Maryland Journal*. She accomplished her task, and at the bottom of the broadsheet she added her name.

Goddard oversaw the task of printing the Declaration of Independence, but its words about liberty and freedom did not include her. In revolutionary America, women did not live as equals with men. Not one man who signed the Declaration even dreamed that women should vote, sit on a jury, or serve in government.

Most people in the Americas and Europe believed that women needed little education beyond being able to read, write, and do simple math. Women's minds, people said, were far too weak to develop great thoughts or hold much knowledge. After all, didn't the Bible say that women were the weaker sex?

From then on, America's women fought a revolution of their own as they challenged the roles that men had written for them. Their battles were many.

Winning the right to vote was one struggle. It took 144 years from the signing of the Declaration of Independence until American women achieved suffrage—the right to go to the polls on Election Day and cast their ballots.

Early suffragists were women who desperately wanted an education and the opportunity to expand their minds. But first they

Suffrage

The word "suffrage" might be new to you. It means "the act of voting in an election." "Franchise" is another word for vote. A person who is allowed to vote is said to be "enfranchised."

The terms "woman suffrage" or "women's suffrage" that you read here refer to the unique topic of a woman's right to vote. That right was not included in the original US Constitution. Each state was allowed to write its own laws about suffrage. In the early days of the United States, voting rights were usually reserved for white men who owned property. By the time the Civil War started in 1861, most states had granted suffrage to all adult white men.

had to overcome their fathers' objections to schooling girls. This story about women's suffrage opens with two of them, Lucy Stone and Elizabeth Cady Stanton. A third, Susan B. Anthony, got the education she wanted, but then she was forbidden to speak out in public against the evils of slavery.

It was time to act. Stone, Stanton, and Anthony gathered up their skirts and their courage and set out to find their voices. Though their paths diverged over the years, all three knew in their souls that American women must win what was rightfully theirs: the right to vote. Only then could they take a full role as citizens of the United States of America.

★ Lucy Stone and her daughter,
Alice Stone Blackwell.

Library of Congress LC-USZ62-135241

Lucy Stone

ON A FARM near West Brookfield, Massachusetts, lived a young girl named Lucy Stone, the eighth of nine children. In 1820s Massachusetts, farm life was hard. Lucy and her sisters and brothers labored along with their parents; they cared for livestock and grew food. Like so many American women in the early 1800s, Lucy's mother, Hannah, saw four of her nine children die.

For Hannah and other women who worked on farms, life could be bleak and cheerless. The work seemed to never end. They nursed their babies, kept their little ones from falling into fireplaces or down wells, cooked meals over open fires, cleaned, raised chickens, grew vegetables, and did the family's washing and ironing—which itself took two days each week.

As a farm woman, Hannah Stone lived a rigid life with her duties spelled out for her. No one questioned how hard she worked; it was expected. The night before

Lucy was born, her father was away from home, and Hannah had milked all the cows. When baby Lucy arrived, Hannah despaired. "A woman's lot [*life*] is so hard," she often said to her daughters. Lucy Stone grew up hearing that she should have been a boy.

Hannah's husband, Francis Stone, worked hard on the farm as well, but Lucy feared her harsh, unbending father. Francis Stone was a drunk who slapped his children around. "There was only one will in my family and it was my father's," Lucy wrote.

Francis Stone tried to make a better life as he moved up from pounding cowhides in a tannery to running a 145-acre farm. Like other Americans, he had hopes that his sons would do better than he had. The farmer toiled to ensure that his sons went away to school in Maine, and he paid their tuition at Amherst College. But Francis Stone did not have the same goals in mind for his daughters. In Lucy's day, few fathers did.

A Woman's Lot

Lucy, like her brothers, grew up learning how to read and do math, but she was not treated in the same way. In the 1820s, most "book learn-

★ **A young Lucy Stone.** Library of Congress LC-USZ6-2055

ing" for girls took place at home, crammed in with all the other duties of each day. Only a few towns in Massachusetts had established public schools, so boys like Lucy's brothers went to private schools in towns or left home to attend private academies. From there, the most promising—and those whose fathers would pay—studied at college to become doctors, lawyers, or ministers.

On Sundays, Lucy and her family sat in hard pews in the Congregational church in West Brookfield, listening to long-winded sermons. These were the days of America's "Great Awakening," when religious fervor swept across the young nation. From the shores of the Atlantic to the Mississippi River, crowds gathered to hear preachers urge them to save their souls. Thunderous ministers, the celebrities of their day, drew people from far and wide.

Children like Lucy heard American churchmen preach about personal salvation from church pulpits in cities and towns and wooden platforms erected in big tents at camp meetings. To get into heaven, roared the ministers, children and adults must accept Jesus Christ as their savior by welcoming him into their hearts. Thousands of people answered the call.

The converts, glowing with new faith, resolved to live as better people and to improve life for others. Their plans to reform American

Craft Your Own Soap

EVEN as Americans moved from a nation of farmers to a land of city dwellers, housewives still made their own soap. Women saved grease left over from cooking meats like bacon by pouring it into a can. The grease had to be remelted over a fire before being processed into soap.

Like other women, suffragists had clothes to wash and dishes to clean. Lucy Stone's recipes for hard and soft soap appeared in the *Woman Suffrage Cook Book*, published in 1890.

Try your hand at soap making. Fortunately, you won't need clean grease or a can of potash. Potash, or "lye," is a chemical compound made from ashes that can burn your skin.

You'll Need
➤ Adult helper
➤ Metal cookie cutters
➤ Cookie sheet
➤ Bar of castile or Ivory soap
➤ Cheese grater
➤ Cutting board
➤ Mixing bowl
➤ Water
➤ Wooden spoon
➤ Measuring spoons
➤ ½–1 teaspoon vanilla or lemon extract
(the kind used in baking)

To start, place several cookie cutters on a baking sheet. Set aside.

Grate a bar of soap using the cheese grater. It's easier to grate if you rest the grater on the cutting board. Pour the grated soap into the bowl.

Add 1 tablespoon of water and mix it into the soap flakes lightly with the spoon. For fragrance, start by adding ½ teaspoon of extract to the mixture. Smell it to see if the scent is strong enough for your taste. If not, add a little more extract until you like the scent.

Use the spoon to gather the mixture into a big ball. Now for some fun: use your hand to

knead the mixture until the soap pieces stick together.

When the soap mixture has the consistency of thick dough, use your fingers to mold it into the cookie cutters. If you wish, heap the soap over the cutters, as shown.

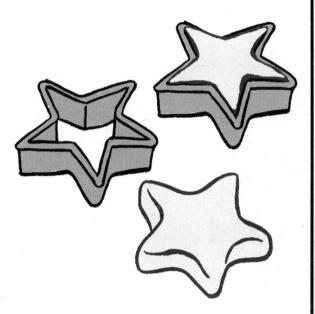

Repeat the process until you have used up all of the mixture. Set the molded soap aside for three days to harden.

Push the soap out of the cookie cutters. Or leave it in and give your soap-and-cookie cutters to your friends as gifts.

life led in two directions. The first was the temperance movement, whose members tried to ban people from drinking alcohol such as whiskey and rum. The other movement for reform was called "abolition." Its goal was to abolish—put an end to—slavery in the United States.

Lucy Stone was impressed by a strong-voiced abolitionist named William Lloyd Garrison. To most Americans, Garrison was a dangerous radical because he demanded an immediate end to slavery. Garrison published his views in his newspaper, *The Liberator*, which found its way into many homes.

Garrison was hated not just in the South but also in the North. As late at 1837, New Yorkers held slaves, so even some Northerners sympathized with Southern slaveholders.

Garrison and other abolitionists toured New England and the Mid-Atlantic states, speaking in churches and lecture halls to curious audiences. People like Lucy Stone looked forward to these meetings, a favorite way for folks to find entertainment during long winter nights.

★ **Abolitionists hoped to put a stop to slavery in the United States. This woodcut was created in 1837, when Lucy Stone attended antislavery lectures.** Library of Congress LC-USZ62-44265

Shall a Woman Speak?

LECTURE GOERS were shocked when two sisters took the stage to speak to the mixed audiences of men and women. They were Angelina and Sarah Grimké, whose Southern father, a rich plantation owner and judge, owned slaves. The sisters hated the idea that anyone, including their father, could own other human beings.

First Sarah, and later Angelina, took the drastic step of leaving home and moving north to Philadelphia. There they became Quakers, who took a very open view of women's rights. Like men, Quaker women were free to speak openly during their times of worship.

Angelina and Sarah learned to speak their minds. The Southern sisters then took things further and went on tour to speak about abolition in public meetings. At this point, even their fellow Quakers frowned when the Grimké women spoke in public.

Angelina Grimké asked for a chance to lecture about slavery in Congregational churches across New England, but church leaders—including Lucy's—hated the idea. When the church in West Brookfield held a meeting to discuss Grimké's request, Lucy Stone was there. Then Josiah Henshaw, a brave young deacon, allowed a woman to speak publicly about abolition. Furious, Lucy's minister and others decided to act against him. The young man was tried in a religious court held in Lucy's West Brookfield church.

Now in her late teens and teaching school, Lucy Stone attended the trial. A vote was called, and Lucy dared to raise her hand in favor of the open-minded Henshaw. She, too, shocked the people around her, and her minister scolded her in front of everyone.

Lucy wondered why the Bible said women should not speak in church. Perhaps, she thought, the Bible had been translated incorrectly from its earlier Greek and Latin versions. Lucy decided that she would learn both ancient languages and find out for herself.

More than anything, Lucy Stone wanted to go to college. In the 1840s, only one was open to women, and that was a frontier college, Oberlin, in far-off Ohio. Until the 1830s, not one college in the United States had admitted women—then Oberlin allowed them to walk through its doors. Lucy Stone's father

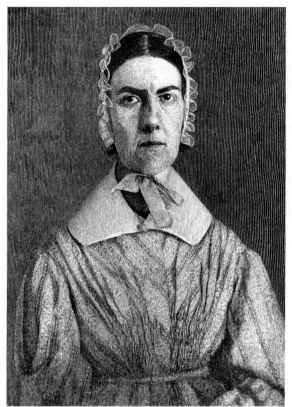

★ **The Quaker sisters Sarah and Angelina Grimké spoke openly against the evils of slavery.**
Library of Congress LC-USZ61-1608, LC-USZ61-1609

provided a perfect example of how difficult it was for young women to get a college education. Francis Stone refused to pay even one dollar of tuition, so Lucy decided to pay for it herself. Now called "Miss Stone," she taught school for $16 a month (half of what a male teacher was paid), stitched shoes, and peddled berries and chestnuts in the farmers' market.

Stone started saving for college when she was 16, and it took nine years before she had the $70 she needed to enter Oberlin in 1843. (Today, that $70 would equal about $1,600.) The journey to Ohio was a 500-mile adventure by railroad and then by ship across Lake Erie from Buffalo to Cleveland. To conserve her hard-earned cash, Stone did not pay for a bed. Instead, she slept atop her trunk on the ship's deck under the stars.

At Oberlin, Stone continued to speak her mind. But even at open-minded Oberlin, she stood out from the other women students. Hats gave her headaches, so she wouldn't wear them—which meant she had to sit in the back at church. She wanted to join her fellow students in debate—answer questions and make speeches in formal meetings—but women could not take part.

Moreover, Stone supported William Lloyd Garrison and hung a picture of him on her wall. Stone hated slavery, and she ached to speak in public to persuade others to become abolition-ists. But as a woman, Stone could not speak in mixed company, only to groups of women like her. To Lucy Stone, this tradition was wrong.

When Stone was about to graduate from Oberlin, her sister wrote to her, saying, "Father says you better come home and get a schoolhouse." But Stone had no plans to teach school. She had decided to step out from her traditional woman's role and go on the road.

Lucy Stone had bigger plans: to earn her living on lecture tours by speaking out against slavery and for women. How, she asked herself, could she read about enslaved mothers and their daughters and not try to help them? If she didn't speak out against slavery, then she was as guilty as anyone.

It wasn't easy. Everywhere she went, Stone ran into roadblocks. The Anti-Slavery Society, her employer, wanted her to focus on abolition, so she made her antislavery speeches on weekends. During the week, when audiences were smaller, Stone felt free to talk about women's rights.

She expected an assortment of boos and cat-calls, but when Stone took the podium to speak, people pelted her with trash. Once she was hit in the head with a prayer book. Another time, angry men forced a window open during the cold of winter, pushed in a hose, and sprayed Stone with icy water. She wrapped a shawl around her shoulders and kept on speaking.

When onlookers set their eyes on Lucy, they saw a modest, quiet woman, now in her early 30s. She wore her hair in a plain, no-nonsense style that covered her ears. A newspaper described her looks and how she spoke: "Mrs. Stone is small, with dark-brown hair, gray eyes, fine teeth, florid [*too red*] complexion, and has a sparkling, intellectual face. Her voice is soft, clear, and musical; her manner in speaking is quiet, making but few gestures, and usually standing in one place."

At times Stone felt alone, trying to convince others to share her ideas. Women, she declared, deserved better lives. In courts of justice and in politics, women deserved the same rights as men. At church and in matters of morality, women deserved equality and respect. At home, women should live as equals with their husbands.

Stone's musical voice charmed her listeners. Stone also charmed a young man named Henry Blackwell. Stone was surprised at Henry's attention. All her life, she had worked to get an education and then to become a lecturer. Lucy Stone did not envision herself as someone's wife. She did not plan to marry anyone.

But Henry Blackwell had a different plan. When he met Stone, he fell madly in love. Henry admired strong women. Seven years younger than Stone, Henry came from a big family and had remarkable sisters. Every Blackwell sister followed her passion, and not one got married.

Two of Henry's sisters, Elizabeth and Emily, became doctors. Others were poets, journalists, and authors. To the Blackwell girls, marriage meant giving up their independence, and they chose lives as single women. Dr. Elizabeth Blackwell spoke for them all when she declared that "true work is perfect freedom and full satisfaction."

Stone took years before she agreed to marry Henry Blackwell. She kept putting off her answer until Blackwell proved himself to her. Finally, he did. In September 1854, Blackwell got word that a little girl, a slave, was traveling with her owners on a train through the Midwest. Blackwell jumped on the train in Salem, Ohio, scooped up the little girl, and took her away to freedom. Henry Blackwell had proved himself a fitting husband for Lucy Stone.

The following May, the wedding of Lucy Stone and Henry Blackwell made headlines and shocked Americans. During their ceremony, Henry spoke about marriage and how it favored husbands over wives. Henry declared that, as Lucy's husband, he would have no legal right to her earnings, her property, or her "person" (body).

Lucy dismayed her family and friends when she refused to take Henry's last name and kept her own. Her decision was so outrageous that in later years other women who followed her example were called "Lucy Stoners."

When Lucy and Henry's daughter was born two years later, her name also reflected her parents' progressive attitude. The happy parents named her Alice Stone Blackwell.

Henry Blackwell went on to become a businessman. He hoped to make enough money to retire and live a life of reading and following his interests, but he often failed at work. Meanwhile, Lucy Stone kept soldiering on, speaking out against slavery and for women's rights.

Stone was single-minded in her devotion to her work. Fortunately, there were other women who felt like she did. In 1848, a group of them would find their voices and speak out.

A Woman's Place

MANY AMERICANS accepted the idea of educating girls—as long as they returned home after they finished college or became teachers. Teaching was considered appropriate for women; after all, women were in charge of keeping America's children on the "straight and narrow" path to clean, moral living. Teachers were tasked with building strong character among their students.

Teachers did not need a college degree in order to work in a classroom. Only a few women went to Oberlin or the other women's colleges that sprang up between 1830 and 1860. To be sure, most of those lucky college women had the backing of their parents, especially their fathers. In the 1800s, fathers ruled their wives and children. A father's rule was law, and the laws of the United States agreed.

In early 1800s America, no women had the right to vote. Still, unmarried women had far more rights than married women had. Women without husbands could choose to work and spend their wages as they liked. They were free to buy and sell land, buildings, and other kinds of property, as well as to enter into business agreements by signing contracts. They could go to court and sue someone if that person damaged their property or hurt them. Likewise, if they damaged property, they could be sued.

But the moment a woman got married, all that changed. Under the law, a woman and everything she owned—from cows and barns to the combs in her hair and the shoes on her feet—became her husband's property. Her money became his, and any pay that she earned now went to her husband.

These laws reached back far into history. Long before Great Britain founded colonies in North America, Englishmen lived under common law, a system that had been in place for hundreds of years. Now many states used common law as the model for their own rules about marriage.

American lawyers got their information about common law from thick leather volumes of *Commentaries on the Laws of England*. Written in the 1760s by William Blackstone, a British lawyer, the books explained England's common law in clear terms that were easy to understand.

Although Blackstone wasn't always accurate, many states in the United States followed his ideas about marriage. To Blackstone, a married couple was a single "being," and the husband stood in charge of his wife. His words, written in England decades earlier, defined a married woman's place in American society.

> *By marriage, the husband and wife are one person in law: that is, the very being or legal existence of the woman is suspended during the marriage, or at least is incorporated and consolidated into that of the husband: under whose wing, protection, and cover, she performs everything.*

Blackstone's ideas were supported by another powerful influence—churches and synagogues. Protestant, Roman Catholic, and Jewish traditions declared that wives must obey their husbands. The Bible's first creation story said that God made both Adam and Eve in God's own image, but other Bible passages seemed to say that women were inferior creatures.

Ministers, priests, and rabbis based their beliefs on these Bible passages, the foundation for ancient Jewish laws governing marriage. Bible stories talked about the men who led the 12 Tribes of Israel and stood over their wives, children, and slaves. Women were actually given by their fathers to their husbands. In synagogues, men and older boys could speak during worship, but women and girls sat hidden behind a screen.

★ **ABOVE: An engraving shows American reformers with three major documents: the Bible, the Constitution, and Blackstone's *Commentaries on the Laws of England.*** Library of Congress LC-USZ62-90671

★ **RIGHT: Sir William Blackstone.** Library of Congress LC-DIG-pga-03621

9

In Christian churches, there were similar ideas about the women's roles. Few Christians questioned the established order of Creation described in the Bible's second creation story. First came God, who gave the first man, Adam, dominion—or "authority"—over his wife, Eve. God also gave Adam dominion over their children and other living things. Then the Bible said that Eve became the first human to sin when she disobeyed God in the Garden of Eden. She ate a forbidden apple from the Tree of Knowledge, and she gave Adam a bite as well.

From then on, churchmen claimed that all women were "daughters of Eve" who tempted hapless men into breaking God's laws. Christians read from the Letter of Paul to the Ephesians, which said, "Wives, be subject to your husbands." Except among Quakers, women could not serve as clergy or speak openly in church.

Plainly, it was a man's world in 1800s America. Wives and daughters were ruled by husbands and fathers. Fathers decided how much schooling their daughters should have and whether it was worth paying for. Only a few young girls challenged their fathers' rigid ideas about the roles of women. Two such girls, born three years apart in the 1810s, stood out from the rest. One was Lucy Stone. The other was Elizabeth Cady.

This engraving, printed on a tobacco label in 1869, pictured Eve tempting Adam. Library of Congress LC-USZ62-37639

2

Elizabeth Cady Stanton

WHILE LUCY Stone was growing up on a Massachusetts farm, Elizabeth Cady was living a far different girlhood in upstate New York. Elizabeth's father, Daniel Cady, a successful lawyer and judge, provided a comfortable middle-class home for his wife and children in Johnstown, New York.

Elizabeth grew up in a warm house with plenty of food to eat and clothes to wear, and she went to school with all the other boys and girls in town. Hired men and women helped with the work at home, and a black slave named Peter kept an eye on Elizabeth and the other Cadys. With her mop of curly blond hair and skirts short enough to move freely, Elizabeth ran the streets of Johnstown with her siblings and friends.

Elizabeth's mother, Margaret, married when she was 17. Over the next 25 years of her life, she gave birth to 11 children. By the time Margaret Cady had her last baby at the age of 44, the family had lost six children. In the early 1800s, proper medical care still lay far off in the future. Doctors did not have medicines to treat diseases, so babies and children died from measles, whooping cough, and scarlet fever. In 1830, a family with 10 children could expect that three or four of them would die while still young.

Fate seemed to frown on Judge Cady and his wife. In their day, families looked forward to having sons to follow in their fathers' footsteps. Sons carried on their fathers' work as well as the family name when they married and became fathers themselves. The young Cady children who died were all boys. Only one of Elizabeth's brothers, Eleazar, lived long enough to go away to college. Eleazar was the pride of his father's heart, and Judge Cady looked forward to his son's return to "read law" in his father's office.

Then Eleazar got sick and died. The Cady home fell into mourning. Again, Daniel and Margaret Cady had to bury a son, but first they laid out his body in a coffin in their parlor. Elizabeth looked back on these terrible days when she was an old woman:

I still recall, too, going into the large darkened parlor to see my brother, and finding *the casket, mirrors, and pictures all draped in white, and my father seated by his side, pale and immovable. As he took no notice of me after standing a long while, I climbed upon his knee, when he mechanically put his arm about me and, with my head resting against his beating heart, we both sat in silence, he thinking of the wreck of all his hopes in the loss of a dear son, and I wondering what could be said or done to fill the void in his breast. At length he heaved a deep sigh and said: "Oh my daughter, I wish you were a boy!"*

Her father's words cut Elizabeth to her very soul. From then on, she set out to prove to her father that she was as good as any boy. She went to the stable and learned to ride the wildest horses possible. At school, she surpassed nearly every boy in her class and took home a school prize in Greek to show her father.

But no matter how difficult the task or how well she mastered it, Elizabeth could not replace a son. Judge Cady was a man of his times. He could think that it was only a pity that Elizabeth was a girl. Women had no place outside their homes. There was no need for a woman to go to college or learn a profession.

Elizabeth chafed under these rules that society had set down for her, but her brainpower kept on growing. She left home for school at the newly opened Troy Female Seminary, one of many secondary schools just for girls that sprang up in the early 1800s. There she continued her study of Latin, Greek, mathematics, science, and literature.

Elizabeth admired Emma Willard, her headmistress, who had founded the challenging girls-only school. Willard planned to prove that young women could study the same tough subjects as young men without hurting their health or ability to have babies, as some doctors feared.

Once Elizabeth finished school, she returned home to live a proper young lady's life. As friends from school came and went,

★ **Elizabeth Cady attended the Troy Female Seminary. Girls could not go to college.**

she enjoyed outings on horseback in the summer and sledding parties in the winter. Now referred to as "Miss Cady," she took herself to her father's law office, where she read Blackstone's *Commentaries* and argued about them with the young men who worked as law clerks for her father.

Elizabeth Cady had strong opinions, especially about Blackstone's views on rights for women. She and her sister Margaret also enjoyed competing with young men's ideas. Nothing pleased her more than a long argument with them on women's equality.

For Elizabeth Cady, the game was on, and she prepared by studying the books they read and the games they played. Only one goal was in her mind: "to make those young men recognize my equality." She learned to play chess and was satisfied that, "after losing a few games of chess, my opponent talked less of masculine superiority."

Elizabeth especially enjoyed the company of her brother-in-law Edward Bayard, who had married her older sister Tryphena. Edward enjoyed the company of Elizabeth and her friends. He challenged them to think deeply about what they had learned at school. He asked lots of questions, and when they answered, he challenged them with even more. They "discoursed" on law, philosophy, political economy, history, and poetry.

Together they read many novels. During long winter evenings in front of the fire, Edward Bayard read aloud from thrilling tales written by Sir Walter Scott, James Fenimore Cooper, and Charles Dickens. Dickens's popular books arrived chapter by chapter in magazines from England, "leaving us," Elizabeth wrote, "in suspense at the most critical point of the story."

Each year Elizabeth looked forward to her visits to Cousin Gerrit Smith and his wife. In a lovely autumn of 1839, before winter set in and made travel difficult, Elizabeth journeyed to the Smith estate in Peterboro, New York.

Gerrit Smith was a gentleman and a scholar. The Smiths had a house full of company, including a crowd of young men and women who liked to have fun. They didn't know that Gerrit and Elizabeth Smith had several escaping slaves hidden away on their property. The Smith household was a stop on the Underground Railroad.

One afternoon, Gerrit Smith called Elizabeth and the other young women away from the parlor. He led them to the third floor of the house. There sat a young girl, age 18—she was an escaped slave who had run all the way from New Orleans. Elizabeth noted that she was a "quadroon," which is a mixed-race woman who has three white grandparents and one African grandparent. Elizabeth recorded what happened next.

★ **Elizabeth Cady Stanton.**

Play a Game of Blindman's Bluff

As a girl, Elizabeth Cady treasured the year's three best holidays. As an old woman, she looked back on those days of joy and wrote about Christmastime. Stanton and her friends played blindman's *buff*, but today it's more commonly known as blindman's *bluff*.

The great events of the year were the Christmas holidays, the Fourth of July, and "general training," as the review of the county militia was then called. The winter gala days are associated, in my memory, with hanging up stockings and with turkeys, mince pies, sweet cider, and sleigh rides by moonlight. My earliest recollections of those happy days, when schools were closed, books laid aside, and unusual liberties allowed, center in that large cellar kitchen to which I have already referred. There we spent many winter evenings in uninterrupted enjoyment. A large fireplace with huge logs shed warmth and cheerfulness around. In one corner sat Peter sawing his violin, while our youthful neighbors danced with us and played blindman's buff almost every evening during the vacation.

Now grab your friends and play a game of blindman's bluff.

You'll Need
➤ Large open room or an open outdoor area
➤ Five or more players
➤ Scarf or blindfold

Decide on the boundaries for your game and clear the area of obstacles like throw rugs or chairs.

Choose someone to be "It," who puts on the blindfold. Turn It around several times. It then counts out loud to 25; everyone scatters until It says "Stop!" It wanders about, trying to tag players out. A player's feet must not move, but the player is allowed to twist and turn to avoid being tagged. Play until everyone has been tagged—and until everyone has a chance to be It.

★ A game of blindman's bluff.

At last, opening a door, he ushered us into a large room in the center of which sat a beautiful quadroon girl about eighteen years of age. Addressing her he said: "Harriet, I have brought all my young cousins to see you. I want you to make good abolitionists of them by telling them the history of your life—what you have seen and suffered in slavery." …

For two hours we listened to the sad story of her childhood and youth separated from all her family and sold for her beauty in a New Orleans market when but fourteen years of age.… We all wept together as she talked, and when Cousin Gerrit returned to summon us away we needed no further education to make us earnest abolitionists.

Among the visitors to Peterboro was a young man in his 20s named Henry Stanton. A keen abolitionist, the dark-haired, blue-eyed Stanton made his living on the lecture circuit. Believing that Henry Stanton was engaged, Elizabeth spoke eagerly with Henry about his experiences. She felt free of the awkward, tongue-tied nerves that young people sometimes feel when they meet an attractive person.

However, Stanton was not engaged, and he began to court Elizabeth. Not long thereafter, Henry Stanton asked Elizabeth to marry him. As she expected, her father stood firmly against the marriage. How, Judge Cady asked Elizabeth, could a lecturer without a real job expect to support a wife?

For a time, Elizabeth ignored her father's questions, but she broke the engagement. Then, just as quickly, Henry Stanton made plans to sail to London for the World Anti-Slavery conference the next summer. Elizabeth did not want an ocean to roll between them, so she changed her mind and married Henry Stanton in May 1840.

★ In 1838, Elizabeth Cady's cousin Gerrit Smith was present at an antislavery society meeting in Philadelphia when a mob burned its brand-new building to the ground. Library of Congress LC-USZ62-1951

Like Lucy Stone, Elizabeth Cady "obstinately refused to obey" her new husband, "one with whom I supposed I was entering in an equal relation." Henry accepted this giant step away from tradition, and their minister dropped the promise to obey from Elizabeth's marriage vows. Unlike Lucy Stone, Elizabeth did take her husband's last name as her own.

The Stantons sailed to England, where both Elizabeth and Henry planned to serve as delegates to the antislavery conference. When they arrived to take their seats, they gasped in surprise. Their English hosts, many of whom were churchmen, refused to seat women as delegates to the convention. Elizabeth had to take a seat behind a low bar hung with a curtain.

The English ministers "seemed to have God and his angels especially in their care and keeping and were in agony lest the women should do or say something to shock the heavenly hosts," Elizabeth Stanton scoffed. She wondered what the heroines of the Old Testament would have said about the conference. "Deborah... and Esther might have questioned the propriety of calling it a World's Convention, when only half of humanity was represented there."

Some of the world's most influential women listened in the back section of the room—all were abolitionists. The Americans Angelina and Sarah Grimké were there, along with

Disconnect and Reconnect

KIDS today spend their evenings far differently than young people in Elizabeth Cady's day. Listen to how she spent them:

The long winter evenings thus passed pleasantly, Mr. Bayard alternately talking and reading aloud [Sir Walter] Scott... and [Charles] Dickens, whose works were just then coming out in numbers from week to week, always leaving us in suspense at the most critical point of the story. Our readings were varied with recitations, music, dancing, and games.

What do you do at night and on weekends? How much time do you spend with your family? Do you hang out together? Or do you spend your time on a computer or listening to music through earphones?

Here's the challenge: Can your family turn off the TV, computers, video games, and smartphones after dinner—and all weekend—for *a whole week*? What can you do instead?

Brainstorm some ideas. Check out the activities in this book: play blindman's bluff, perform in a readers' theater, make an oil lamp, paint some china, or start a scrapbook. Read aloud together or host a tea party.

When the week's up, think about what felt different and why. What have you learned about how you use your free time? What did you learn about spending time with others face-to-face?

★ **As men debated on stage at the World Anti-Slavery Conference in 1841, the women had to sit behind them and were refused a chance to speak.** Library of Congress 1841 LC-USZ62-133477

other famous reformers. Among the Englishwoman was Anne Isabella Byron, wife of the famed poet Lord Byron and a member of England's upper class. Humiliated and chagrined as Stanton and these ladies felt, more than anything they scorned the shallow reasons men gave for separating them.

One Quaker woman caught Stanton's eye. The petite, bonneted Lucretia Mott, an American like Stanton, had journeyed to London with her husband, James. Lucretia Mott was a full generation older than Stanton, and Stanton admired the older woman's wisdom. As a couple, James and Lucretia Mott had made a name among abolitionists, and Mott also spoke out on women's rights.

During their days in London, Elizabeth Stanton and Lucretia Mott discovered they were of one mind—they thought that women deserved to be treated equally with men. As

Lucretia Mott

A teacher when she turned 16 in 1809, Lucretia Mott discovered that she was paid half of what a man made. To Mott, such treatment was a sin against God. "[T]he injustice of this was so apparent that I early resolved to claim for my sex all that an impartial Creator had bestowed," Mott wrote.

She went on to become a Quaker minister, free to speak when Quaker men and women gathered to worship. However, when Lucretia Mott chose to speak to men in public in Philadelphia about the evils of slavery, a mob burned down the building where she lectured.

Mott's speeches about slavery to mixed groups of women and men went too far, even for her broad-minded Quaker friends. But onward she went, even as she raised six children and hid escaping slaves in their home.

Mott was a stay-at-home mother, like most women in her day, but she resolved to continue improving her mind. The sewing machine had yet to be invented when her children were small. When Mott did the family mending, she "omitted much unnecessary stitching and ornamental work" to squeeze in more time to read.

★ **Lucretia Mott pictured in her Quaker bonnet.**
Library of Congress rbnawsa n3028a

---

the convention adjourned, a new idea buzzed among the participants: "It is about time some demand was made for new liberties for women."

Stanton and Mott walked home arm in arm, as friends did, sharing the events of the day. It was a remarkable moment for Stanton when she and Mott "resolved to hold a convention as soon as we returned home and form a society to advocate the rights of women."

That convention took place eight years later.

Five Cups of Tea

In 1847, the Stantons moved to Seneca Falls, New York, near the tip of Cayuga Lake in the Finger Lakes. By now, Elizabeth was the mother of four children. As was always the case with Henry Stanton, he was too busy with work to help with the move. Elizabeth Stanton, her sister, their five children, and seventeen trunks made a two-day trip by train from Boston. The whole time, Stanton worried that one of the little ones would fall off the platform into the path of a moving steam engine.

She took charge of their new home, a run-down place just outside Seneca Falls, where she hired workers to repair the building. Seneca Falls was not Boston, as Stanton soon realized. She missed the big city with its exciting, reform-minded women and men.

Here in Seneca Falls, a blighted mill town, she could not find good servants to help her with her children, and Henry was always away working. Stanton also realized that she and her husband could easily have a big family, but she was the only one at home to care for their children.

> *To keep a house and grounds in good order, purchase every article for daily use, keep the wardrobes of half a dozen human beings in proper trim, take the children to dentists, shoemakers, and different schools, or find teachers at home altogether made sufficient work to keep one brain busy as well as all the hands I could impress into the service.... I suffered with mental hunger, which, like an empty stomach, is very depressing.*

Things got even worse during the warm weather. Seneca Falls had mosquitoes, and all the children caught malaria after getting bitten. They were sick for three months with chills and fevers. For better or worse, Stanton had to set aside her personal battle for women's rights to take care of her children.

Then Stanton received a welcome invitation to tea. Lucretia Mott was visiting her Quaker friends and relatives in a nearby town. On June 10, 1848, Elizabeth hopped on the train and went to Waterloo for a tea party with four others, including her cousin Elizabeth Smith Miller. This group of "earnest, thoughtful women" listened to her frustration.

"I poured out that day the torrent of my long accumulating discontent with such vehemence and indignation that I stirred myself as well as the rest of the party to do and dare anything," Stanton said later.

That very night, they wrote "the call." The announcement of a Woman's Rights Convention was published in the *Seneca Falls Courier* the next day.

Stanton and another woman, Mary Ann "Lizzie" McClintock, met again before the convention. Taking pens to paper, they wrote a rough draft of a document they called "A Declaration of Sentiments." In clear writing, the two women made their case for women's rights. Their model was close at hand: Stanton and McClintock used the Declaration of Independence as the starting point for their own declarations.

Time for Tea and Talk

CLEVER suffragists knew that one-on-one meetings would help recruit women to "the cause." Often such gatherings took place in their homes, where women could meet each other in comfort and speak openly. Suffragists often did their work while sharing cups of tea and something sweet.

Invite some friends and have a tea party to talk over important issues in your lives. Set a pretty table, round up a teapot and some cups, and add your favorite sweets. Here's how to plan your party. If you wish, serve the suffrage cake shown on pages 59–60.

You'll Need

- Adult helper
- Table
- Tablecloth
- Table decoration
- Napkins
- Dessert plates
- Teacups and saucers
- Forks and teaspoons
- Serving plates
- Assortment of desserts, such as cookies, cake, and fresh fruit
- Sugar bowl and spoon
- Small pitcher
- Milk
- 1 lemon, washed and sliced thin
- Teapot
- Teabags in a flavor you like
- Note cards
- Pencils
- Fun friends who enjoy a good talk

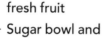

MAKING PREPARATIONS

Set the table with a pretty cloth. Add a simple table decoration—flowers in a vase, a pretty plant, or even a gathering of colorful stones or shells in a bowl.

At each place lay a folded napkin, a dessert plate, a teacup and saucer, a fork, and a spoon. Just before your guests arrive, place serving plates filled with goodies on the table. These will be passed from guest to guest. Add the sugar bowl, a small pitcher of milk, and a plate of lemon slices along with a small fork.

MAKING TEA

To make hot tea, first be sure your teapot is clean. Warm the pot by filling it with hot tap water and set it aside. With an adult's help, fill your teakettle and set it on the stove to boil. The tea water must come to a full boil.

In the old days, people poured hot water over tea leaves right in the pot and then poured the tea through a strainer into their cups. Today, we use teabags—one teabag per person, plus one for the pot.

NOW IT'S TIME TO PARTY

As your guests arrive, give each one a pencil and note card. Ask each guest to write down one topic that he or she would like to share with the group.

Pour and serve the tea to your guests in their teacups. Offer them sugar, lemon, and milk. (Warning: don't use lemon and milk together—the lemon will curdle the milk and make a mess.) Pass around the plates of goodies, and invite your friends to help themselves.

As host, it's your job to keep the conversation going. Ask your guests to share the topics they wrote on their note cards. Be sure that everyone has had a chance to share by the time your tea party is finished.

What kinds of topics did you discuss?

On the morning of July 19, 1848, a crowd packed into the pews of the Wesleyan Chapel in Seneca Falls. Visitors came from all walks of life: educated women like Lucy Stone and Elizabeth Stanton, others who were not as well schooled but just as curious, some open-minded men, and a group of country girls led by a young glove maker named Charlotte Woodward. Like Stone, Woodward did piecework (sewed gloves by hand at home) on the family farm, and, like Stone, she hated the thought of turning her hard-earned income over to the men in her family.

When the meeting opened on July 19, 1848, convention goers were greeted with Stanton and McClintock's Declaration. Its 942 words would rock their world.

The Declaration of Sentiments

ELIZABETH CADY Stanton's Declaration of Sentiments summed up every fact that made women second-class Americans. Stanton echoed Thomas Jefferson's stirring Declaration of Independence against England, but she made his words the words of women everywhere.

We hold these truths to be self-evident: that all men and women are created equal; that they are endowed by their Creator with certain inalienable rights; that among these are life, liberty, and the pursuit of happiness....

The history of mankind is a history of repeated injuries and usurpations on the part of man toward woman, having in direct object the establishment of an absolute tyranny over her. To prove this, let facts be submitted to a candid world.

He has never permitted her to exercise her inalienable right to the elective franchise. [Women could not vote.]

He has compelled her to submit to laws, in the formation of which she had no voice. [Women obeyed laws they did not help to write.]

He has withheld from her rights which are given to the most ignorant and degraded men—both natives and foreigners. [Men denied women the same rights held by uneducated men who were not citizens.]

He has made her, if married, in the eye of the law, civilly dead.

He has taken from her all right in property, even to the wages she earns....

In the covenant of marriage, she is compelled to promise obedience to her husband, he becoming, to all intents and purposes, her master....

He has so framed the laws of divorce...as to be wholly regardless of the happiness of women....

Make a Memory

Y ou might think that scrapbooks are a modern hobby, but pasting pictures, letters, and newspaper clippings into albums was popular among suffragists and others in the 1800s. The Library of Congress—the United States' national storehouse of books, photos, music, and more—has a repository of suffrage scrapbooks. Elizabeth Cady Stanton's cousins, Elizabeth Smith Miller and Anne Fitzhugh Miller, filled seven albums with mementos of their work for the vote. Go online and watch a video called "Catch the Suffragists' Spirit: The Millers' Suffrage Scrapbooks" at http://www.loc.gov/today/cyberlc/feature_wdesc.php?rec=4839.

Now it's your turn to make a memory. Create a scrapbook in which you can store special mementos from your life. To keep things easy to move around, use something you're familiar with, like a loose-leaf notebook.

You'll Need

➤ 2-inch, 3-hole loose-leaf binder with a plastic cover
➤ Heavyweight (24-pound) paper (choose colors you like)
➤ Piece of 3-hole notebook paper and paper punch (or a three-hole punch)
➤ Card stock for making pocket pages (directions are below)
➤ 1-inch masking tape
➤ Scissors
➤ Rubber cement
➤ Assortment of pens, pencils, markers, glitter pens
➤ Anything that helps you preserve a memory, such as photos, newspaper clippings, letters, tickets, postcards, and event programs

To begin, fill your scrapbook with paper. Using the piece of notebook paper as a template,

Advertiser-Gazette.

EDGAR PARKER, Editor.

GENEVA TELEPHONE NO. 51.

Thursday, October, 25, 1906.

—City papers may criticise or comment upon the wearing apparel of Mrs. Elizabeth Smith Miller of Geneva, as much as they please, but the fact remains that she is the sweetest old lady that ever lived, so kind-hearted, so womanly, so rare in all good deeds. Her home is one of quiet refinement and enjoyment, and there she and her daughter, Miss Anne F., pass away their lives, sitting on the east broad veranda overlooking the smooth waters of Seneca Lake, whose ripples lave the shores of their pretty property. Mrs. Miller is now a little past 84 years of age, yet in nice weather, we see her down street nearly every day, with a kindly smile, a pleasant word for everybody. Such women ought to live forever. And her husband, Col. Charles D. Miller, although not a church-going man, had a warm heart beneath his vest—he was sure to give that famous team of bronze sorrels a rest on Sunday always.

★ **Elizabeth Smith Miller pasted a newspaper clipping about herself in one of her scrapbooks.** Library of Congress rbcmil scrp7000601

punch holes in the heavyweight paper. Or use a three-hole paper punch if you have one.

Use the card stock to make pocket pages. Three pieces of card stock make two pocket pages. Start by folding one piece of card stock in half, as shown. Cut along the folded line. Place one full piece of card stock on your work surface. Place a half piece on top, matching three sides.

Cut a piece of masking tape a bit longer than the width of the card stock. Lay the tape upside down on your work surface. Now place the bottom of your pocket page along the tape so that it's half off, half on, as shown. Flip the tape over to the front. Use your fingers to gently seal the

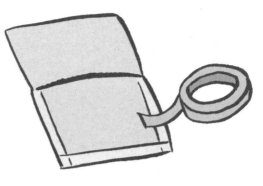

tape along the bottom edge. Trim the ends of the tape even with the card stock.

Repeat the procedure with the sides of the pocket: tape, flip, and seal. Trim the edges into a neat square. Now run your fingers along all the taped edges.

Punch three holes in your pocket page to fit the rings in your scrapbook. You're ready to fill your pocket page with memory-making items!

Finally, make a cover for your binder. Use pictures, cutouts, glitter pens, small flat trinkets—you can even make a collage. Let your imagination fly! Slip your artwork into the plastic cover on the front of the binder.

When you open this scrapbook 50 years from now, what memories do you want jumping out at you? Items that evoke these memories are

the ones you will want to add to your project. By using a binder, you can arrange your memorabilia any way you wish.

One more thing: you get much of your information from the Internet. How are you going to preserve your "e-memories"? You might have to print out e-mails or download copies of articles you read online. There might also be CDs or DVDs for you to include—maybe a thumb drive, too.

Could the Miller sisters ever have imagined that you'd read their scrapbooks by looking at an electronic device? Find them at http://memory.loc.gov/ammem/collections/suffrage/millerscrapbooks. Click on "Scrapbook" on the left-hand side.

After depriving her of all rights as a married woman, if single, and the owner of property, he has taxed her to support a government....

Stanton listed a long series of complaints: women's lack of good jobs, poor pay, no chance to go to college, and no opportunities to serve as ministers. Then she finished with a flourish.

Amelia Bloomer

The outlandish costume that enraged men was invented by Elizabeth Cady Stanton's cousin Elizabeth Miller. However, "bloomers" took their name from a woman who adored wearing them—Amelia Bloomer.

Bloomer started her reform work as a member of the temperance movement, campaigning against the evils of alcoholic drinks. She sat in the audience when Stanton and other

★ **Amelia Bloomer proudly wore bloomers, which were named after her.** Seneca Falls Historical Society

women opened their battle for women's suffrage at Seneca Falls in 1848.

Years ahead of most women in her views, Bloomer launched the *Lily*, a newspaper for women with short stories and articles about temperance and women's rights. Bloomer, who was fiercely independent, wore her "Turkish trousers" everywhere. They were comfortable and convenient. She didn't have to hold them up off muddy streets.

Outraged spectators accused her of "man-

nishness." Bloomer spat back, "I feel no more like a man now than I did in long skirts, unless it be that enjoying more freedom and cutting off the fetters [chains] is to be like a man."

Bloomer married a dedicated Quaker lawyer who believed in women's rights. She was devoted to him, and when he decided to move west, she sold the *Lily* and went with him. Nonetheless, all her life Bloomer fought Victorian views about womanly duties in marriage.

Bloomer asked pointed questions to anyone within earshot. Why was it a woman's "duty" to obey her husband if God had created them equal? If women were expected to raise children to be good moral adults, then why did the law forbid mothers any legal authority over their own children?

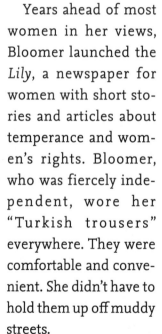

Now, in view of this entire disfranchisement of one-half the people of this country, ... we insist that they have immediate admission to all the rights and privileges which belong to them as citizens of the United States.

The call for women's suffrage—granting women the right to vote—shocked America's reformers. Only one man at Seneca Falls, the abolitionist Frederick Douglass, agreed with Elizabeth Stanton's demand.

For others, both women and men, the thought that women might cast ballots along with men was going too far. Lucretia Mott fretted. "Why, Lizzie, thee will make us ridiculous," she said in the Quaker way of addressing a friend.

Mott was correct, as "Lizzie" knew. The newspapers made fun of Stanton's ideas. All the journals from Maine to Texas called her thoughts "ridiculous." Stanton later wrote about what happened after the Seneca Falls convention:

[S]o pronounced was the popular voice against us, in the parlor, press, and pulpit, that most of the ladies who had attended the convention and signed the declaration, one by one, withdrew their names and influence and joined our persecutors. Our friends gave us the cold shoulder.

Stanton took criticism well. When her cousin Elizabeth Miller designed a new "costume" for women to wear, Stanton eagerly put one on. Her bloomer outfit caused tongues to wag, but Stanton praised its comfort and convenience. She wore bloomers for several years. The costumes caused so much fuss that suffragists finally gave them up. The women decided that there were more important things to accomplish than dress reform.

The bold gathering at Seneca Falls had sparked an idea. Another women's rights convention took place in Rochester, New York, the next month. After that, women in state after state hosted their own meetings to continue their talks. From one small tea party, a nationwide interest in women's suffrage began to grow.

With so many children to care for, Stanton couldn't travel to meet with other women's rights activists. Ideas flowed from her mind easily—but what wouldn't come easily was leaving home. Clearly, Elizabeth Cady Stanton needed help to take her beliefs on the road.

★ When Elizabeth Cady Stanton's daughter Harriot was born, her mother wrote words of joy in having given birth to a girl.

Library of Congress LC-USZ62-48965

3

Susan B. Anthony

To THE good fortune of women everywhere, Elizabeth Cady Stanton got the helping hands she needed. In the early 1850s she met a "stately Quaker girl" named Susan Brownell Anthony. Like Elizabeth, Susan had her roots in New York State and grew up in a big family. But Susan's father, an open-minded Quaker, believed that women should speak their minds in public.

Daniel Anthony ran a textile mill in Battenville, New York, and owned other businesses. He encouraged Susan to develop her mind to become an independent thinker—and not to fear speaking out.

Susan's father also believed in the virtue of hard work. When one of his factory workers was sick, Susan stepped in to work with the other mill girls. As a spooler in her father's factory tending giant spools of cotton thread, Susan worked for two weeks and proudly claimed wages of her own.

As busy as Daniel Anthony was, he also carved out time to work as an abolitionist. Over time, he became more civic-minded and fell out of favor with his Quaker friends. Quakers preached against evil but did not believe they should take part in worldly activities like politics.

During one cold New York winter, a man in the Anthonys' town froze to death. Near his corpse was found an empty whiskey jug, sure evidence of the evil of hard drink. Daniel Anthony was revolted, and he swore never to sell hard liquor in any of his businesses. He joined the crusade for temperance, and when Susan first began her own work as a reformer, she began by taking part in the fight against alcoholic drinks.

A Stately Quaker Girl

SUSAN ANTHONY adored her father and tried to follow his example as she grew up. She learned that complaining about evil was not enough. When she believed that society was wrong, she decided that she must act.

Daniel Anthony proudly sent his daughters to a Quaker boarding school near Philadelphia and traveled there with Susan to enroll her. Her older sister, Guelma, had prospered there, and Daniel Anthony had the same hopes for Susan.

However, despite her joy in studying mathematics and science, Susan had a dreadful experience at the school. The headmistress, a strict Quaker, seemed to single out Susan with biting words. Susan's teacher taunted her in class, mocking her when Susan admitted she did not know the rule for "dotting an *i*."

This teacher embodied the religious education of her own colonial girlhood, when adults believed that children were born wicked and must have their pride driven out of them. Like Lucy Stone and Elizabeth Cady, Susan was a serious girl who worried about her soul and her relationship with God. Over the months, the teacher drove so much poison into Susan's mind that the girl began to doubt herself.

"Perhaps the reason I can not see my own defects is because my heart is hardened," she confessed in her diary. "We were cautioned by our dear Teacher to-day to beware of self-esteem," she added. Instead of building confidence in her sensitive student, Susan's teacher left marks that wounded Susan and kept her from doing her best for many years.

Susan came home from school to find her father's business in ruins. A nationwide financial panic in 1837—when scores of banks and businesses failed and closed their doors—led to an economic depression in 1838. The Anthonys lost the mill, their home, and most of their possessions. Daniel Anthony moved his family to Hardscrabble, New York, a village as bleak as its name.

Susan Anthony needed a job. In May 1839, she struck out on her own to teach briefly in a Quaker school. Over the next few years, "Miss Anthony" taught school. Often she took jobs in schools whose unruly boys had run off their male teachers.

Anthony had a close friend in Aaron McLean, the grandson of her father's business partner. Then, in 1838, Aaron began to court her older sister, Guelma—he had eyes only for her. Anthony never mentioned her feelings in her diary, but she must have felt some regret that she did not make her romantic feelings for him known. Once Aaron married Guelma, Anthony could not share the same easy friendship with him.

To be sure, Anthony was courted by a number of eligible young men and received several proposals of marriage. But Susan B. Anthony was never to meet a man who excited her more than living the life of a single woman out to reform America.

When Anthony was 26, she became a headmistress herself. She moved to Canajoharie, New York, to teach school and began to explore a freer life away from the strict Quaker eyes that always judged her. She wore bright dresses and went dancing, but she took care to balance her life with reform work. She joined the Daughters of Temperance, an antidrinking group. Anthony also planned to work for abolition, but the townspeople in Canajoharie had no use for the antislavery cause.

When her father decided to start an insurance business, Anthony left teaching and came home to run the family farm. Her family was as active as always in New York's reform efforts. On Sunday afternoons, abolitionists like William Lloyd Garrison and a thundering man named Wendell Phillips came calling in the Anthonys' parlor.

Their zeal to end slavery excited Anthony, and she joined the struggle. "What is American slavery?" she asked. "It is the legalized, systematic robbery of the bodies and souls of nearly four millions of men, women, and children. It is the legalized traffic in God's image."

In her diary, she left quiet evidence about taking a stand against slavery. On a summer day in 1861, she "superintended the plowing of the orchard.... The last load of hay is in the barn; all in capital order. Fitted out a fugitive slave for Canada with the help of Harriet Tubman."

The Harriet Tubman whom Anthony mentioned in her diary was none other than the nation's most famous "conductor" on the Underground Railroad. For escaping slaves, reaching Canada meant freedom.

Susan B. Anthony at 26, sitting for her portrait.
The Collection of the Public Library of Cincinnati and Hamilton County

Susan Anthony Finds Her Voice

THESE WERE dangerous days for reformers. Across the United States, slavery was the hot topic in political meetings, church gatherings, and family dinners. Arguments were bitter. Many Americans, even those living in the North, had no problems with slavery and despised abolitionists.

In the North, black Americans, though free under the law, lived second-class lives. They were forbidden to enter libraries, theaters, lectures, hotels, trains, and horse-pulled buses. They were not welcome in most white churches or schools. Many white people feared the idea of emancipation—that slavery would end and black slaves would become free men and women.

Angry mobs could turn up at any point to disrupt a quiet meeting where abolitionists spoke out against the evil of slavery. More than once, Susan B. Anthony faced angry attacks. At one point, a group of men waving pistols and throwing rotten eggs chased Anthony and Samuel May, another abolitionist, off their speaking platform and out into the street. They escaped to a friendly home, but the mob built straw models of Anthony and May and burned them in effigy.

But even as Anthony risked her safety to fight slavery, she found that she could not speak out at all. The "mob," as she called these unruly groups, hated the idea of women speaking in public. She was even more upset when most gentlemen of the educated class agreed with the mob. All too often, when she rose to speak at meetings, the men in charge told her to sit down. Their job was to speak; hers was to sit quietly and learn.

The ongoing fight just to speak in public fueled a fire in Anthony's soul and sparked an idea. In order to make an impact on society, she decided to change society by bringing some measure of fairness into women's lives. Such fairness, she believed, would come if American women could take part in the nation's political arena.

From then on, Susan B. Anthony fought for one reform only: women's suffrage, the right for America's women to vote.

She had found her voice.

Keeping Goddesses in Their Place

LUCY STONE's gritty life as a farm girl contrasted sharply with the lives of girls like Elizabeth Cady Stanton and Susan B. Anthony. Stone watched her father and mother work side by side on the farm along with the rest of their family. However, Stanton's and

★ **Susan B. Anthony was in her mid-40s when this portrait was made.** The Collection of the Public Library of Cincinnati and Hamilton County

Make an Oil Lamp

BEFORE natural gas was piped into homes for nighttime lighting, people depended on oil lamps to read, write, or do handwork at night. When Susan Anthony was a girl, she probably read by a lamp whose fuel came from oil extracted from whale blubber.

Make your own little lamp shine using just a few items. You will need an adult to help out as you create your lamp and light it.

You'll Need

➤ Adult helper
➤ Small clear glass jar with a sturdy metal lid, such as a canning or pickle jar
➤ Candle wicking (sold at hardware and craft stores)
➤ Scissors
➤ Small bowl
➤ Olive oil
➤ Hammer
➤ Large nail
➤ Piece of wood for a work surface
➤ Water
➤ Safety matches
➤ Nonflammable surface such as a metal or glass pan
➤ Long pin

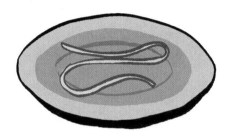

To begin, wash and dry a glass jar. Set aside. Measure the wick to the height of the jar plus one inch and cut with scissors. Place the wick in the small bowl. Pour olive oil over the wick until it's just covered. Allow the oil to soak through the wick for 15 minutes.

To make a hole for the wick, turn the jar lid upside down on a wooden work surface. Use a hammer to drive a nail through the middle of the lid. Be sure the nail pierces the metal completely, but don't hammer the lid to the work surface. Set aside.

When the oil has soaked through the wick, you are ready to assemble your lamp.

Fill the jar half full of water. Now pour olive oil into the jar until it's almost full.

Poke the wick through the jar lid from bottom to top. You want about ½ inch to peek out.

Tightly screw the lid to the jar so that the wick hangs into the olive oil.

Place your lamp on a nonflammable surface. Strike a match and light the wick. It might take a moment to set the wick on fire. (Hint: If your lamp burns only a short time, add more olive oil so that it comes nearly to the top of the jar and try again.)

In time, the wick will burn down, so you will need to use a straight pin to pull up more of the wick from below. But only pull the wick up through the jar top *when it's not burning.*

Turn out the lights and see how well your lamp works. How well could you do homework with just your lamp for light?

Anthony's fathers worked in offices, a new trend in American life.

Stanton and Anthony grew up as members of the middle class. As cities and towns grew in the 1820s and 1830s, middle-class men left home each morning to work somewhere else. Their jobs took them into the hard-hitting, rough-and-tumble environment of American commerce.

For middle- and upper-class American women and girls, life changed, too. Unlike their colonial foremothers, women lived their lives at home, separate from men, running households and raising children. It seemed that women lived in one world and men in another.

America's opinion makers, including doctors, educators, ministers, and newspaper editors, admired this change in women's roles. They prized the ideal woman as a mother and homemaker who lived in a "Cult of Domesticity."

Outside the home, men did the "dirty work" of making money, practicing law or medicine, leading church congregations, or entering politics. Inside the home, women were supposed to make their dwellings calm, clean, and hallowed places.

★ **The Cult of Domesticity praised women's roles as wives, mothers, and keepers of the home.**
The Collection of the Public Library of Cincinnati and Hamilton County

Sarah Josepha Hale

In the mid-1800s, one of America's leading women was Sarah Josepha Hale, a magazine editor whose work reached homes coast-to-coast. Hale's husband had died suddenly, leaving her with five children and no money. Hale needed a job, so she picked up her pen and started to write, first a book of poetry, then a novel.

Hale's talent glowed. In a day when few women held powerful jobs, she won a position as editor of the *American Ladies Magazine*. Hale's clever ideas and strong writing attracted readers. Her success caught the eye of Louis Godey, a publisher who recruited her to join *Godey's Lady's Book*. For 40 years, Hale edited America's top women's magazine.

Along with Godey's famous fashion images, recipes, and housekeeping tips, readers enjoyed stories and poems by Henry Wadsworth Longfellow, Ralph Waldo Emerson, and Edgar Allan Poe. Hale also introduced her readers to Harriet Beecher Stowe, whose book about slavery took America by storm. Stowe, in fact, agreed with Hale on another matter:

American women should be well educated and lead healthy lives.

Godey's Lady's Book was famed for its color illustrations of fashion for women and children. But Hale balked at the pulled-in corsets that gave women fashionable but unhealthy "wasp" waists. (Still, the wasp waist never went out of fashion.)

Hale pushed for her readers to exercise, ride horses, and even to swim, in case they were thrown overboard in a steamboat accident. She applauded modern household improvements—hand-cranked washing machines and rotary eggbeaters to replace the tiresome job of whipping cream with a fork.

Though Hale never asked women to step into the world of men, she prized the value of educating girls. She called for women to become doctors in female medical schools in order to solve another problem. When Hale was a young mother, too many women died in childbirth, too shy to seek help from doctors, who always were men.

★ Sarah Josepha Hale.

In later life, Hale wrote to President Abraham Lincoln with a suggestion that the nation celebrate a new holiday: Thanksgiving. Most of all, Americans today know her as the author of "Mary Had a Little Lamb."

Practice Your Posture

IN the "olden days," girls practiced standing up straight by walking with books balanced on their heads. Certainly that's one way to learn how to stand tall, but today fitness experts agree that a daily dose of exercise is a better choice. In fact, 60 minutes—one hour—of activity every day is recommended for kids. (Are you a couch or computer potato? Do you really spend 60 whole minutes moving each day?)

The US government has a health-and-fitness website just for kids called BAM—Body and Mind. On this website you'll find all sorts of ideas for ways to keep active for an hour each day—everything from ballet to basketball, from judo to ping-pong to yoga. Check it out at www.bam.gov.

Just for fun, try the old-fashioned way to practice good posture. It's not as easy as you might think!

You'll Need

➤ Medium-sized hardcover book
➤ Space to practice walking

Read this recommendation of a teacher written in the 1850s. Put the book on your head, stand straight, drop your arms, and practice walking.

[G]reat advance in [exercise] might be made, if, whilst practising a slow marching walk with the foot lifted up and the step made from toe to heel, a heavy book, or other proportionate weight were carried on the head—the arms, in the meanwhile,

★ **Boys and girls were expected to stand up straight in Victorian times, when good posture was a sign of good background.** iStockphoto, copyright © Linda Steward

hanging gracefully down. This should be practised till the weight can be carried for a considerable time without falling or moving—the spine in such case, in order to balance the weight, assuming a most erect and graceful posture.

This writer believed that young women who practiced their posture would surely be "modest in demeanour [behavior] and gentle in speech." Do you agree ?

Do you think you could keep this posture every time you walk?

Women's roles were strictly defined. They were charged with teaching their children about God and reading God's word in the Bible. It was a mother's duty to raise her sons to follow their fathers into the workplace. The same rules demanded that mothers teach their daughters the virtues of becoming loving wives and good mothers.

Not just men accepted this view of American life in the early and mid-1800s. Many—if not most—women agreed that they had no business going to college or working at jobs. Of course, working-class women had to work as servants or as mill girls in textile factories to manufacture cloth. But the middle-class American woman, one whose husband could pay the bills, stayed inside her sphere, an invisible glass ball. She became an ideal, a domestic goddess.

Even a women's magazine—run by a woman—praised the homemaker as America's model woman. *Godey's Lady's Book* and its strong-minded editor, Sarah Josepha Hale, declared, "Our men are sufficiently money-making. Let us keep our women and children from contagion [*sin and vice*] as long as possible."

Hale popularized the Cult of Domesticity as if it were a brand of soap or shampoo. From

★ **Women in the 1840s wore tight corsets to create wasp waists featured in** *Godey's Lady's Book.*

factory girls to rich women in their boudoirs, 150,000 American women read *Godey's Lady's Book.*

4

Finding a Platform

AS A new decade opened in 1850, the movement for women's rights pushed forward. Yet for the most part, Americans scoffed at the fledging efforts among women reformers. Meanwhile, abolitionists kept working toward an end to slavery, but the South rallied to protect its way of life. By the late 1850s, it seemed likely that the United States could split in two over the issue of slavery.

Sometimes reformers fought with each other to bring Americans' attention to their efforts. Clearly, the antislavery movement and the women's rights movement were rivals for people's attention.

However, three women helped draw the public into both groups. These remarkable reformers were Harriet Tubman, Sojourner Truth, and Harriet Beecher Stowe. Because they were not men, they stood out. Tubman, Truth, and Stowe gave American women a rightful place on the public stage.

★ OPPOSITE: Scenes from *Uncle Tom's Cabin* brought the issue of slavery to white Americans as nothing else had.
Library of Congress LC-USZ62-1351

Harriet Tubman

HARRIET TUBMAN was born a slave but ended up not only escaping to freedom but leading more than 300 other slaves to free lives as well. Tubman started life on a Maryland plantation as Araminta Ross but changed her name to Harriet, her mother's name. As a young girl in the 1820s, Harriet served as a house slave in her master's home. But when she reached her teens, she was sent to do the backbreaking work of a field hand.

A feisty young woman, Harriet tried to protect a fellow slave from an angry overseer. The overseer threw a two-pound weight at the slave but missed and hit Harriet in the head. Ever after, from time to time she would pass out and experience blackouts.

In her teens Harriet was permitted to take a husband, a free black man named John Tubman. Then her master died, and Harriet Tubman faced being sold. Like all slaves who lived in Maryland and Virginia, Tubman dreaded being sold "down the river" to the Deep South, where slaves were often worked to death. Tubman trusted no one, not even her husband. Giving no inkling of her plans, Tubman slipped away from the plantation and followed the Underground Railroad north to safety. It was 1849.

Freedom was not enough for Tubman, however, and she became the Underground Railroad's most-famed conductor. With her eyes on the North Star and a price on her head, Tubman made journey after journey back to the South to deliver more people to freedom, including her aged parents.

Abolitionists cheered Tubman's accomplishments, as did Lucretia Mott, who understood that Harriet Tubman was a powerful symbol. Tubman was a woman doing the kind of hard work traditionally considered "man's work."

Sojourner Truth Speaks for Women

A GENERATION before Harriet Tubman was born a slave in Maryland, another girl was born a slave in the North. In 1797, little Isabella Baumfree, a black child, was the property of a Dutch American who lived in New York. As in the South, slaves in New York were bought and sold like horses or cows. When she was about 20 years old, her owner forced Isabella to marry another slave whom she didn't love, and she gave birth to five children.

★ As a former slave, Harriet Tubman did not know her birthday, but she stood for this portrait sometime between the ages of 40 and 55. Library of Congress LC-USZ62-7816

In 1827, the state of New York passed an antislavery law, and Isabella claimed her right to be free. Her master did not agree, so she left her home. Listening to the voices in her head that had spoken to her ever since she was a girl, Isabella became a preacher. She changed her name to Sojourner Truth. (To sojourn means "to stay someplace for a short time.")

Sojourner Truth lived out her name in New England, where she traveled the roads to camp meetings and lectures. Truth stood out, not just because of her color and her gender. She stood nearly six feet tall in a day when few men topped out at more than five feet nine inches.

In 1851, Truth traveled from New England to east-central Ohio, where a women's rights convention was planned at Akron. When she entered the first session in a church, she caused a stir. Not everyone welcomed a black woman walking into a church, recalled Frances Gage, an abolitionist.

The leaders of the movement trembled on seeing a tall, gaunt black woman in a gray dress and white turban, surmounted with an uncouth sunbonnet, march deliberately into the church, walk with the air of a queen up the aisle, and take her seat upon the pulpit steps. A buzz of disapprobation was heard all over the house, and there fell on the lis-

tening ear, "An abolition affair!" "Woman's rights and n——s!" "I told you so!"

Fearful conventioneers came to Gage, worried that Truth might actually speak. The next morning, a series of ministers took their turns at the pulpit. Methodist, Baptist, Episcopalian, Presbyterian, and Universalist men declared their opposition to women's rights. They offered the usual excuses.

One churchman preached that men were more intelligent than women. Another stated that woman came second to man because Jesus was male. Yet another minister added that because of Eve's sin in the Garden of Eden, all women were equally sinful.

Once the ministers had finished their speeches, Frances Gage allowed Sojourner Truth to take the pulpit. Even the people staring through the windows could hear Truth's ringing words. Gage recalled Truth's speech:

"Well, children, where there is so much racket there must be something out of kilter. I think that 'twixt the negroes of the South and the women at the North, all talking about rights, the white men will be in a fix pretty soon. But what's all this here talking about?

"That man over there says that women need to be helped into carriages, and lifted over ditches, and to have the best place

★ **Wherever she went, Sojourner Truth wore a white cap. She did not know her age when she sat for this portrait in 1864.** Library of Congress LC-USZ62-119343

everywhere. Nobody ever helps me into car-
riages, or over mud-puddles, or gives me any
best place!"

Gage then recalled,

And raising herself to her full height, and her
voice to a pitch like rolling thunder, [Truth]
asked, "And ain't I a woman? Look at me!
Look at my arm! (and she bared her right
arm to the shoulder, showing her tremen-
dous muscular power) I have ploughed and
planted, and gathered into barns, and no
man could head me! And ain't I a woman?
I could work as much and eat as much as a
man—when I could get it—and bear the
lash as well! And ain't I a woman? I have
borne thirteen children, and seen most all
sold off to slavery, and when I cried out with
my mother's grief, none but Jesus heard me!
And ain't I a woman?"

Gage continued with Truth's comments
about women's minds:

"Then they talk about this thing in the head;
what's this they call it? ("Intellect," whis-
pered some one near.) "That's it, honey.
What's that got to do with women's rights or
negroes' rights? If my cup won't hold but a
pint, and yours holds a quart, wouldn't you

be mean not to let me have my little half
measure full?"

Gage wrote more about Sojourner Truth's
rebuke at the ministers.

And she [Truth] pointed her significant
finger, and sent a keen glance at the minister
who had made the argument. The cheering
was long and loud.
"Then that little man in black there, he
says women can't have as much rights as
men, 'cause Christ wasn't a woman! Where
did your Christ come from?"
Rolling thunder couldn't have stilled that
crowd, as did those deep, wonderful tones,
as she stood there with outstretched arms
and eyes of fire. Raising her voice still louder,
she repeated,
"Where did your Christ come from? From
God and a woman! Man had nothing to do
with Him." …
Turning again to another objector, she
took up the defense of Mother Eve, and she
ended by asserting:
"If the first woman God ever made was
strong enough to turn the world upside
down all alone, these women together ought
to be able to turn it back, and get it right
side up again! And now they is asking to do
it, the men better let them."

Find Polaris, the North Star

THE North Star is an unusual and helpful star. It certainly proved useful to Harriet Tubman as she led escaping slaves north to freedom.

Officially named "Polaris," the star appears directly over the North Pole. Unlike all other stars that move in the night sky, Polaris seems to stand still. Since ancient times, sailors have looked to Polaris to help them calculate their latitude—how far north they are from the equator.

Several constellations appear to rotate around Polaris. Among these star groups are Ursa Major (known as the Great Bear) and Ursa Minor (known as the Small Bear). People usually call these constellations the Big Dipper and the Little Dipper. "Dipper" is a name for a long-handled drinking cup.

With one look skyward, Harriet Tubman could find the North Star and make sure that she was heading in the correct direction. But in a night sky filled with stars, the North Star isn't especially bright. Tubman knew a trick for spotting it. First, she had to find the Big Dipper.

★ RIGHT: The northern sky at night in July. Tubman used the Big Dipper, easy to find in the night sky, as a useful way to locate the North Star, which isn't especially bright.

How did Tubman find Polaris? Discover for yourself.

You'll Need
➤ Clear, cloudless night
➤ Open space for stargazing (best away from the city)

Head outside on a clear night and look skyward to find the Big Dipper in the north. Even if you live in a city with bright lights, you should be able to find the Big Dipper.

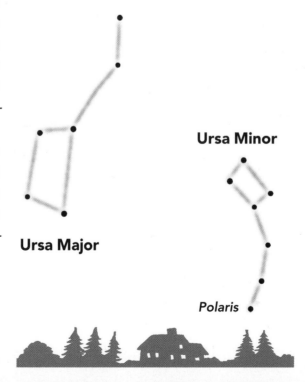

Ursa Minor

Ursa Major

Polaris

Do you see the "drinking cup"? Depending on the time of year, it might be on its side or upside down. Now find the two stars that make up the outside end of the cup, as shown:

Starting at the bottom of the cup, draw an imaginary line through both stars and continue your way onward. Your imaginary line will point to Polaris, the North Star. Can you see it?

Polaris is the last star on the handle of the Little Dipper. Now look for the Little Dipper. It faces the Big Dipper but is much fainter and can be hard to spot.

Bonus question: Why is the North Star named Polaris?

Polaris gets its name from polus, the ancient Latin word for "pole."

Long continued cheering greeted this. "Obliged to you for hearing me, and now old Sojourner ain't got nothing more to say."

In one short speech, Sojourner Truth had summed up every good reason for women to stand forever equal with men.

Harriet Beecher Stowe

IN 1851, a homemaker-author busied herself writing installments of an exciting novel about slavery in the American South. Harriet Beecher Stowe, a member of a prominent, outspoken family, had lived in Cincinnati, just

Elizabeth Packard

In 1860, an Illinois woman was imprisoned for disagreeing with her husband. Elizabeth Packard, the wife of a minister with strict beliefs, challenged her husband's preaching and left his church.

Her husband decided that if his wife disagreed with him, she must be insane. The laws in Illinois gave him power over her body and medical care, so Reverend Packard had her locked up in an "insane asylum," a dreadful place that was meant to house people with mental illness. Mrs. Packard spent three years there until she was sent home, where her husband locked her in an upstairs room and boarded the window.

Friends managed to find Elizabeth Packard a lawyer, and they went to court.

There, Reverend Packard used his narrow views about God to justify his treatment of his perfectly healthy wife. It took a jury—all members of which were men—only seven minutes to declare that Elizabeth Packard was not insane.

When Reverend Packard saw that he would lose the case, he took Elizabeth's clothes and their children and left Illinois. It took another five years until Elizabeth Packard could see her children again. By then, they were mostly grown up.

Elizabeth Packard spent the rest of her long life fighting the Illinois law that her husband had used against her. She also won married women in Illinois the right to own property in their own names. Still, she didn't paint herself as a suffragist. The

★ **Elizabeth Packard was imprisoned in a mental hospital because she disagreed with her husband.**

clever Mrs. Packard disguised herself as an "anti" in order to win acceptance by male legislators who despised the idea of women voting.

across the Ohio River from the slave state of Kentucky. As a young wife and mother, Harriet saw slavery at work with her own eyes, and she met families who had escaped over the winter ice to freedom in Ohio. Stowe's harrowing story drew her readers' attention to the shattered lives of enslaved people.

From her desk in her family home in Maine, Stowe dispatched handwritten chapters of *Uncle Tom's Cabin* to the *National Era* magazine. For a woman author to be so widely read was remarkable in American life. From the first page forward, readers were captured by her strong story that tugged at their hearts.

Stowe caught her readers' attention in the first chapter. Two men, one a gentleman slaveholder named Shelby and the other a trader called Haley, discuss the sale of three slaves. First they talk about an elderly slave named Tom. Then they argue about two others: a little boy named Harry and his lovely mother, Eliza. The trader asks about Eliza:

"Come, how will you trade about the gal?— what shall I say for her—what'll you take?"

"Mr. Haley, she is not to be sold," said Shelby. "My wife would not part with her for her weight in gold."

"Ay, ay! women always say such things, cause they ha'nt no sort of calculation [no sense about money]. Just show 'em how many watches, feathers, and trinkets, one's weight in gold would buy, and that alters the case, I reckon."

"I tell you, Haley, this must not be spoken of; I say no, and I mean no," said Shelby, decidedly.

"Well, you'll let me have the boy, though," said the trader; "you must own I've come down pretty handsomely for him."

In those few lines, Stowe set the scene for a classic tale. Published as a book in 1852, *Uncle Tom's Cabin* sold an astounding 300,000 copies. Her scenes astounded Americans, too. In the North, Stowe became a heroine. In the South, it was a different story. Her book was banned, and Stowe's name was poison. Stowe's message against slavery enfuriated Southern men, who went on to question her womanliness because she wrote it.

Harriet Beecher Stowe became so well-known she was invited to the White House in 1862 to meet the tall and dignified president, Abraham Lincoln. Lincoln's greeting to the petite author has become a legend. War between North and South had begun the year before, and when Lincoln took her hand, he said, "So you are the little lady who started the Civil War."

★ **This portrait of Harriet Beecher Stowe was taken in 1880, 30 years after her book took America by storm.** Library of Congress LC-USZ62-11212

5

Sidetracked by War

THE CONTROVERSY over the right of Southerners to own slaves grew more heated as the United States moved toward war in the 1850s and early 1860s. Life in the North contrasted sharply with life in Southern society. The Northern states included growing cities, where people worked in factories, small towns, and thousands of small farms that were worked by their owners.

In the South, however, life was very different. Its economy depended on the success of giant tracts of farmland called plantations. White plantation owners depended on the labor of their slaves to grow their crops of cotton, tobacco, and sugar. Even small farms used slaves they owned or rented. A few large cities dotted the South, but they were not the same bustling centers of manufacturing and trade that were spreading from New England into the Midwest and down the Pacific coast.

★ OPPOSITE: Sometimes families lived with soldier husbands and fathers in camps away from Civil War battlefields.
Library of Congress LC-USZC4-7983

45

As the young nation pushed west into the territories of Texas, Missouri, Kansas, and Nebraska, slavery became a hot issue. Americans added new stars to their flag and wondered: Would these states allow slavery or not? "Free soilers" called for new states to forbid slavery, a demand that made Southerners choke. The labor of slaves protected the South's way of life.

When the Republican Party won the election of 1860 and Abraham Lincoln became president, people in the South roared ever louder. Lincoln was not an abolitionist, but the new president did not believe that slavery should spread farther in the West.

Civil War

FROM VIRGINIA south to Florida and west to Texas, Southerners began to speak about forming a nation of their own. One by one, beginning with South Carolina in December 1860, Southern states seceded—withdrew—from the United States to form the Confederate States of America. By April the next spring, the two sides were at war. Northerners fought to preserve the Union, and Southerners fought to protect their right to live as a separate nation.

Over four bloody years, the two sides battled. With double the population and its factories and farms to supply its soldiers, the North held a huge advantage over the South. Even so, the war dragged on.

The cost in human lives shocked everyone. One out of two casualties ended in the death of a soldier. If a soldier were shot, luck was not on his side. More than likely, he would die from his wounds. Of the 1.5 million soldiers who fought for the North, nearly 360,000 died and 275,000 were injured. Among the

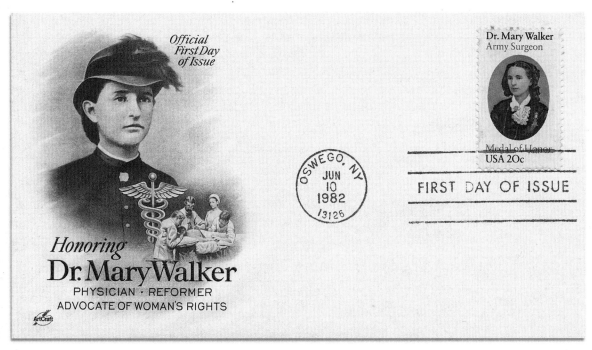

★ **A "first day cover" of a postage stamp honored Mary Walker, a woman who cared for soldiers and was captured during the Civil War.** United States Post Office

South's 800,000 soldiers, some 258,000 died and another 225,000 were wounded.

The hatred between North and South overshadowed every other issue, including the matter of equality for women. In both North and South, women of the upper and middle classes did what they could to support their fighting men. They held social events like teas and balls to raise money for their armies. They also knitted bandages and gloves, sewed blankets and uniforms, and marshaled collections of food to ship to the front.

As the war moved on, it became clear that families of ordinary soldiers who had been drafted into the army were suffering on the home front. It was up to the man of the house to send home his pay. Many soldiers didn't, and their families went hungry. Again, women stepped up to help out these poor families with food to fill hungry children and clothing to keep them warm during long bitter winters.

In time, women went to war themselves, delivering vital supplies to field hospitals near the lines of battle. At first, they weren't welcomed. Male doctors and surgeons doubted that ladies could withstand the blood and gore of these primitive hospitals, where the surgeon's solution to a shattered leg was usually to amputate it.

However, a quiet teacher named Clara Barton changed their thinking. Barton, shy by nature but also caring, saw her wounded students returning from fighting for the Union and decided to deliver supplies right to the front lines. Once there, she stopped to care for wounded soldiers; she cleaned their

★ In 1861, "the ladies of New York" met in a big hall to organize a society to make clothes and lint bandages and to furnish nurses for the Northern army. Library of Congress LC-USZ62-132138

Clara Barton

wounds, changed their bandages, or just held their hands. Her valuable work soon changed the minds of army doctors, and they began to welcome women's help as nurses. Years later, Clara Barton went on to found the International Red Cross.

★ **An old stamp honored Clara Barton, who pioneered women's work as nurses during the Civil War.** United States Post Office

Constitutional Amendments

When the Founding Fathers wrote the Constitution, they planned it as a living document. They realized that, over time, the Constitution would require changes as American life moved on.

Article V of the Constitution describes the amendment process. Amendments can be introduced either in Congress or by a constitutional convention of 34 states. (Amendments are usually introduced by members of Congress.)

An amendment must be approved by a two-thirds majority vote in both the US Senate and the House of Represen-

tatives. Then the amendment is sent to the 50 states for approval in a process called ratification. Thirty-eight state legislatures are required to ratify an amendment.

The best-known amendments are the first 10, which we know as the Bill of Rights. Another well-known amendment, the 18th Amendment, banned the manufacture and drinking of alcoholic beverages in 1919. The 21st Amendment repealed that ban in 1933. In 1971, the 26th Amendment changed the national voting age from 21 to 18.

Setting Suffrage Aside

For the time, Elizabeth Cady Stanton and Susan B. Anthony set aside their drive for women's suffrage to do war work for the Union. They joined hands with abolitionists who, despite the war, still had to press for President Lincoln to declare emancipation and end slavery once and for all.

In a campaign of their own, Stanton and Anthony formed the Women's Loyal National League and organized a petition drive. Petitions were one of the few legal documents a woman could sign, and thousands penned their names to statements calling for the president to abolish slavery.

In the end, 300,000 women and men signed the petitions. The president signed the Emancipation Proclamation in January 1863, setting free the slaves in the Confederate South. (Slavery did not become illegal across the United States until the 13th Amendment abolished it after the Civil War.)

Stanton, Anthony, and their fellow suffragists had a vision. They felt certain that once the war was over and the country reunited, America's leaders would recognize women's war work and reward them with the right to vote.

In April 1865, the terrible war ended as the Confederate general Robert E. Lee surrendered his sword to the Union general Ulysses

★ **A national magazine showed women aiding Union soldiers during the Civil War.**
Library of Congress LC-USZ62-102383, LC-USZ62-102384

S. Grant. Now suffragists had something to look forward to. The US Constitution would need a new amendment, its 14th.

Elizabeth Cady Stanton and Susan B. Anthony expected that the 14th Amendment would guarantee the right to vote to newly freed male slaves and to women both white and black. Surely, they thought, bright days for American women lay ahead.

6

One Step Forward, Two Steps Back

STANTON AND Anthony were wrong. Though the war was over and the slaves had been freed, abolitionists protested that two million free black men did not have the right to vote. Clearly, the US Constitution needed an update—a 14th Amendment. With that goal in mind, members of the Antislavery Society elected a new president, Wendell Phillips.

Phillips and Elizabeth Stanton were close friends, and he had always backed her quest for votes for women. Phillips wrote his first speech, in which he laid out his plans. Stanton expected that Phillips would include women, as well as freed slaves, in the new amendment.

★ OPPOSITE: This drawing on a piece of music shows an artist's take on the suffrage movement in 1869.

Library of Congress musmisc.awho002

But as Stanton listened to Phillips's inaugural speech, she bristled. Wendell Phillips had changed his mind about the timing of women's suffrage, and his words burned Stanton's heart. "I say 'One question at a time.' This is the negro's hour," Phillips declared. Phillips and most of his friends felt that black men should have the vote immediately. Women could wait.

Radical Republicans in Congress, who favored rights for black men, also backed the 14th Amendment. It was a matter of politics, Republicans against Democrats. After the Civil War, the Republican Party held power in both the House of Representatives and the Senate. As former Confederate states wrote new constitutions and were admitted back into the Union, it was clear that they would be controlled by the Democratic Party.

In order to keep Democrats out of power, Republicans wrote the 14th Amendment with two million black men in mind: men who would be happy to support Republicans in the heavily Democratic South.

The opening lines of the 14th Amendment stated that former slaves were now American citizens:

All persons born or naturalized in the United States, and subject to the jurisdiction thereof, are citizens of the United States and of the State wherein they reside.

As suffragists read the next section of the 14th Amendment, their alarm grew. For the first time ever, the word "male" appeared in the US Constitution.

★ **This engraving celebrated the new 15th Amendment, which granted suffrage to former male slaves. Neither black nor white women were given the right to vote.** Library of Congress LC-DIG-pga-03453

It was plain to see that the Constitution, the nation's most important document, made women second-class citizens. So, in 1866, Stanton and Anthony regrouped and founded the American Equal Rights Association. They invited former abolitionists to help fight for votes for women and newly freed slaves.

Congress passed the 14th Amendment in July 1868—a great victory—and the document went to the state legislatures to be ratified. Even so, the 14th Amendment did not guarantee black men a right to vote. Therefore, a group called the Radical Republicans proposed a 15th Amendment. This amendment said that states could not deny voting according to "race, color, or previous condition of servitude [*slavery*]." Nothing mentioned women and their voting rights.

Elizabeth Stanton and Susan Anthony were outraged. How could the Constitution give the vote to men, former slaves who could not read or write, when well educated, cultured women like themselves could not? From then on, Stanton and Anthony felt that the vote should be reserved for educated people.

Other news frustrated them. In New York, the state legislature had backtracked on the Married Woman's Property Act. Once again, only fathers—not mothers—held legal guardianship of their children. It seemed to Anthony that the rush to give the vote to black men would overwhelm women's chances to win votes of their own.

A Questionable Partner

In 1867 Stanton, Anthony, and Lucy Stone headed west to Kansas. There they joined Clarina I. H. Nichol, a Kansan well-known for her strong views on women's rights. In the fall election, men across Kansas (all white, of course) would vote on the issue of suffrage for both blacks and women. The suffragists had work to do.

Many Kansans echoed the same views that held fast in the East. "It is time for the Negro to have the vote," they heard. "If women get the vote, they'll take away our taverns and our liquor," was another complaint. Others griped about the "outsiders" who had come to Kansas to stir up trouble. Then, with just two months until Election Day, Elizabeth Stanton and Susan Anthony gained an unexpected backer—an unsavory man named George Francis Train.

The flamboyant Train wore lavender goatskin gloves and had his eye on one day becoming president. A self-made man, Train did business in real estate and railroads. Train had a mouth and a reputation as loud as his fancy clothes. In a time when people freely used

★ **George Francis Train pictured with his famous lavender gloves.**

Picture Yourself as a Victorian

WHEN we look at a photo of Susan B. Anthony with her tight lips and black dresses, it's hard to imagine her as a living woman with more energy than three people put together. As you view pictures from the 1800s, do you think of their subjects as "real" people?

★ Susan B. Anthony wore black, but her dresses were of fine quality and detail. Often she added a red shawl when it was chilly.

Library of Congress LC-USZ62-23933

In Anthony's time, camera film needed a fairly long exposure to light, sometimes as long as 10 or 15 seconds. If people moved, their image would blur. That's why they didn't smile in photos—or it might be they were hiding their bad teeth.

Can you imagine yourself as a Victorian girl or boy? Dress up and take your picture—Victorian-style! If you are lucky enough to have an older relative with a trunk full of vintage clothes, ask if you may use them. Otherwise, search through a thrift store to find pieces for your outfit.

You'll Need
➤ Dress-up clothes—skirts, blouses, and suits
➤ Accessories—handkerchiefs, hats, shawls, scarves, purses, umbrellas, and canes
➤ Props—chairs, desks, and tables
➤ Camera
➤ Helper to take your picture
➤ Computer
➤ High-quality, textured printing paper
➤ Brown construction paper
➤ Rubber cement

Let your imagination roam as you plan your outfit. Study the photos in this book for ideas. Think about how you will style your hair. Plan the setting for your photo. Will you stand or sit? Will anything else be in your picture? How will you hold your hands and arms?

Adjust the settings on your camera to take pictures in "sepia" tones. Sepia is the brown color you see in many old-fashioned photographs. Many digital cameras have settings to take pictures this way.

When it's time for your "photo shoot," ask your helper to take your picture using different poses. Remember: *Don't* smile!

Download the pictures onto a computer and study the results. Which do you like best? If you weren't able to set your camera to take the pictures in sepia colors, use a photo-editing program to make the adjustments on the computer.

Print out your favorite shots on the high-quality paper. Dab the corners with a bit of rubber cement and mount them on the construction paper. Look at your photos. Can you imagine yourself as a young person in the 1800s?

hateful words to talk about black Americans, Train talked about people of color in the crudest possible terms.

However, George Train believed that women should have the right to vote, so Elizabeth Stanton and Susan Anthony welcomed his help and his money. Even better, Train was a media whiz, and he had a suggestion. Why not start a newspaper to build support for suffrage? Anthony jumped at the idea, and the *Revolution*, the first suffragist newspaper, appeared with the tagline "Men their rights and nothing more; women their rights and nothing less."

The *Revolution* was unlike any other women's publication. Besides the usual articles on homemaking and child care, the *Revolution* gave readers news about real women doing active things in American life. Articles reported on women in all walks of life, from the very few professionals like doctors to factory women organizing labor unions in search of better pay and workplaces.

But then Anthony went too far. In the *Revolution*, she linked the American Equal Rights Association directly to George Train.

Lucy Stone was thunderstruck that Susan and Elizabeth would join forces with the likes of George Train. "I am utterly disgusted and vexed," she wrote to a fellow suffragist. "[O]ur grand cause is dragged in [Train's] bad name—all without my knowledge."

Former abolitionists agreed. William Lloyd Garrison, long a friend to Stanton and Anthony, was "mortified and astonished beyond measure in seeing Elizabeth Cady Stanton and Susan B. Anthony travelling about the country with that harlequin [joker] and semi-lunatic George Francis Train."

Most felt that Stanton and Anthony had put on blinders in the way wagon drivers blinkered their horses with eye flaps to keep them looking straight ahead. Anthony could not see why so many in her circle were upset. She fought back

★ **This 1870 illustration shows the unusual sight of women in anatomy class in an all-female medical school.** Library of Congress USZ62-2053

ACTIVITY

Stage a Readers' Theater for Suffrage

MANY plays about suffragists have appeared onstage. You and a few friends can produce a play of your own by staging a readers' theater. The National Archives, which houses famous documents and records that make up US history, has a play on its website.

The play is titled *Failure Is Impossible*, named for Susan B. Anthony's famous statement. It features a narrator and three readers who play the roles of 15 women and men who worked for suffrage. From Abigail Adams to Carrie Chapman Catt, the play gives an overview of the suffrage story.

You'll Need
➤ You and three friends
➤ Copies of *Failure Is Impossible* (available at www.archives.gov /education/lessons/woman-suffrage /script.html)

Download and print out four copies of the play. Read through it and assign parts to each reader. Each person should practice alone at first. When you are ready, practice reading the play from beginning to end.

Get ready for "opening night"! Gather an audience and perform *Failure Is Impossible*. Perhaps you can perform it for your class at school or in a community center.

with stinging words that ripped old friendships apart. "I AM the Equal Rights Association. Not one of you amounts to shucks [*a "hill of beans"*] except for me." She said to Lucy Stone, "I know what is the matter with you. It is envy, and spleen, and hate, because I have a paper [the *Revolution*] and you have not."

These women, once so united in their work for women's rights, fought like wolves. They held secret meetings, wrote hush-hush letters, and told tales behind each others' backs. With their eyes fixed on the prize of winning women the vote, Anthony and Stanton dropped their old friendships and battled onward. It seemed they did not care how many friends they lost.

In the coming months, the movement for women's suffrage split in two. Suffragists like Lucy Stone and Henry Blackwell, former abolitionists, and other moderates backed the 15th Amendment. Let the black man vote, they felt. Surely votes for women would follow.

With this outlook, Stone, Blackwell, and another suffragist named Julia Ward Howe launched the American Woman Suffrage Association (AWSA) in 1869. Stone moved from New York to Boston to live closer to other moderate suffragists.

Stone's long, patient view of things underscored the American Woman Suffrage Association. The group planned its strategy: grassroots campaigns in every state. AWSA worked from

Victoria Claflin Woodhull

When Victoria Claflin Woodhull became the first woman to run for president of the United States in 1872, Stanton and Anthony applauded her bold vision. Dynamic yet offbeat, Woodhull held a broad, open view of what women's lives could become. She wanted women to do everything that men did.

Born in 1838, Victoria Claflin grew up the daughter of spiritualists, a shady couple who said they were in touch with the dead. At 15, she married a Dr. Woodhull and had two children. But as her alcoholic husband came and went, Victoria decided to make a change.

Tiny, blond, and bright, Victoria Woodhull charmed her way into high society. She and her sister Tennessee started a women's newspaper and became the first women to act as stockbrokers. Like their parents, the sisters held séances and claimed they could communicate between this world and the next.

Woodhull's radical views upset the stodgy Victorians around her and overshadowed her successes. Among other extreme ideas, Woodhull believed that couples should be free to divorce, a notion that infuriated most people. In real life, she practiced what she preached, marrying a second husband before legally divorcing the first.

As Woodhull's fame grew, her extreme opinions about women's rights drew Elizabeth Stanton like a moth to a candle. Susan Anthony, however, held back. She feared that Woodhull was out for her own gain, out to "run our craft [*boat*] into her port and no other."

Without asking Anthony, Stanton invited Victoria Woodhull to speak at a NWSA meeting. Anthony got angry and Stanton withdrew, leaving Anthony in charge. When Victoria Woodhull showed up to take the podium, Anthony sent her away. Woodhull appeared again the following night and started speaking. When she wouldn't stop, Anthony turned out the lights.

Susan B. Anthony and Elizabeth Cady Stanton never agreed about Victoria Woodhull. Woodhull herself moved to England, where she took a third husband, lectured, wrote books, and gave her wealth away to good causes. She died in 1927.

★ **A woman thought to be Victoria Woodhull lobbied members of the House of Representatives to give women the vote.**
Library of Congress LC-USZ62-2023

the bottom up by recruiting women and men to push for suffrage where they lived. From there, citizen suffragists could point their efforts at their state legislators. With enough influence, states would have no choice but to give women the vote. State by state—this would be the AWSA's way of doing things.

To boost AWSA's efforts, Stone launched her own newspaper, the *Woman's Journal*, to compete with the *Revolution*. Like the *Revolution*, the *Woman's Journal* covered topics that interested middle-class housewives in the 1870s. The *Journal*, however, took a much quieter tone that appealed to a wider group of women.

Susan B. Anthony and Elizabeth Cady Stanton formed their own National Woman Suffrage Association (NWSA) in New York City. They campaigned against the 15th Amendment and continued to press for a constitutional amendment to give American women the vote once and for all. Nothing less would ever satisfy them.

Eventually Anthony and Stanton dumped George Train and moved the publishing offices of the *Revolution* out of his building. Men were no longer allowed to join their group, in sharp contrast to Lucy Stone's suffrage organization.

Despite all their hard work and good intentions, the *Revolution* folded in three years. Its extreme outlook did not appeal to most Americans. The newspaper could not keep enough readers and advertisers to run a profit. Susan B. Anthony had invested $10,000 of her own money—a giant sum—in her paper. Later she had to pay it back by lecturing and writing. In contrast to the *Revolution*, the *Woman's Journal*, with its moderate views and popular tone, stayed in circulation until 1931, bringing its message to homes across America.

The split in the suffrage movement offered a lesson to anyone in the United States who was thinking about reform. There would be two sides, with different ideas, about how to right something that was wrong. One side—Elizabeth Cady Stanton, Susan B. Anthony, and NWSA—was far ahead of its time. On the other side were moderates like Lucy Stone and AWSA, who stood for the larger—and quieter—group of reformers whose views on suffrage were acceptable to more Americans. Numbers proved their case; AWSA always counted on far more members and a larger treasury than NWSA.

AWSA and NWSA stayed divided for 20 years.

A Wound That Would Not Heal

THESE WERE the days of Victorian America, when society followed a set of rules named for

Bake a Cake with Suffrage Frosting

THE *Woman Suffrage Cook Book* offers many cake recipes like this one.

The cookbook's editor took for granted that her readers knew how to bake cakes. (Today's cooks—not so sure!) Girls had to learn the steps, and there were books to teach them. One was *Six Little Cooks: or, Aunt Jane's Cooking Class,* a girls' book published in 1877. Read and see how times have changed:

Accordingly the class was called together for a general examination and review.... Then Aunt Jane began...

"What is the first thing you must provide yourselves with when you are going to cook?"

"Clean hands and nails and tidy hair."

"Next?"

"Clean aprons."

"What must you have in the kitchen?"

"A good fire and plenty of hot water."

"What is the rule about dishes and other utensils?"

"To use just as few as we possibly can, and manage so as to take the same one for several things when it won't spoil the taste of what we're making."

"What ought you to do with flour?"

"Sift it, always."

"What must you do in breaking eggs?"

"Break each one into a separate saucer before you put it with the rest."

"And if you accidentally get one in that isn't fresh?"

"Throw away the whole dishful!"

"How about separating the yolks and whites?"

"Break them separate for all kinds of delicate cake, or for anything that is to be very light. But the recipes generally give you directions."

"Is there anything where it is best not to separate them?"

"Baked custards, and gingerbread, and such things."

"Rather indefinite, but no matter. When must you use 'cooking butter'?"

"Never!"

"And skim-milk?"

"Never when you can get any other."

"In making cake, what do you do first?"

"Rub the butter to a cream, and then put the sugar with it, and then the yolks of the eggs (after you have beaten them)."

"How do you generally put in white of egg?"

"Alternately with the flour, unless you have different directions."

"And soda?"

"The last thing, except flour, and then you must bake anything immediately and not let it stand."

"How do you prepare the soda?"

"Dissolve it in something—warm water, or sometimes, vinegar."

"And cream tartar or baking-powder?"

"Sift it with the flour."

Wow! Today's mixes make cake baking much easier and taste just as good. However, homemade frosting still beats anything you find in a can. Several recipes for chocolate frosting appear in the *Woman Suffrage Cook Book*. Bake a cake, ice it with frosting you make yourself, and see if you agree.

You'll Need
➤ Adult helper

For the cake:
➤ Cake mix of your choice (yellow, white, or chocolate)
➤ Ingredients listed on the back of the box, such as water and eggs
➤ 9-by-13-inch baking pan
➤ Large mixing bowl
➤ Electric mixer
➤ Measuring cups

For the icing:
➤ Grater
➤ 2 squares unsweetened baking chocolate
➤ Small bowl
➤ ¼ cup water
➤ Saucepan
➤ Wooden spoon
➤ 1 cup white sugar
➤ Spatula

Bake the cake in the baking pan by following the directions on the box. When the cake comes out of the oven, allow it to cool for several hours in the pan on a cooling rack.

To make the icing, grate the chocolate into the small bowl. Then bring the ¼ cup of water to boil in the saucepan. Turn down the heat to very low. Using the wooden spoon, mix the sugar and grated chocolate into the water until they dissolve.

Keep cooking the icing at very low heat for 10 minutes. The icing will bubble up from the center. Stir it often to keep it from burning. Using a spatula, spread the icing over the top and sides of the cooled cake. Then cut the cake into serving-size pieces.

Britain's prim, upstanding Queen Victoria. Women were expected to dress modestly and follow strict standards of behavior. Unpleasant topics were not to be discussed openly.

As Victorian women, Lucy Stone and others kept quiet in public about touchy issues that affected women and girls. Like so many wives, Stone understood heartbreak when Henry Blackwell strayed from their marriage and saw another woman. Stone decided not to leave her marriage, keeping to Victorian ways and her growing belief that divorce was wrong. (In time, Blackwell returned.)

But to Elizabeth Cady Stanton and Susan B. Anthony, hushing up problems in the Victorian way was no solution at all. They talked—loudly—about all sorts of issues, topics such as wife beating, divorce, and the right of women to use birth control to manage the number of children they bore.

Such concerns were not considered proper talk in public. Victorians did not discuss diseases such as cancer or mental illness. It was unthinkable for a middle- or upper-class woman to appear in public when she was pregnant.

Young women often entered marriage not understanding "where babies came from." Though families had fewer children than earlier in the century, large families were still expected and respected. All the same, as in the early 1800s, the grim truth was that women often died giving birth. Many women worked themselves into early deaths on lonely farms or Western homesteads. In cemeteries, it was common to see a headstone for one man flanked by the graves of two or even three wives.

Wonderful Wyoming Women

Two thousand miles from and 21 years after the first Woman's Rights Convention at Seneca Falls, the state of Wyoming granted suffrage to women. Ever since, Wyoming's nickname, the "Equality State," has stuck.

When Wyoming's governor signed the law in 1869, a Wyoming woman named Esther Morris cheered. Morris had started her working life as a seamstress and bonnet maker in New York, but when she married a man with three sons, they moved west during a gold rush.

The following year, Morris was appointed justice of the peace in South Pass, which made her the first woman in the United States to serve in public office. Six feet tall and strong featured, Morris heard cases as she sat on a bench in her log cabin. Her grown sons served as court clerks. Her first order was for everyone to keep their shooting irons outside.

Historians disagree whether Morris worked for suffrage, but there is no doubt that she held court in Wyoming. She heard criminal cases (most involving men who were charged with assault) and civic cases (such as when people fell into debt). As a judge, she also married people, including a scandalous couple who had lived together for two years "without benefit of clergy or the law."

Esther Morris wanted to run in the next election to keep her job. But neither political party would nominate her, and she stepped down. She was proud to have passed the test of a woman's ability to hold public office. The same year she ran her courtroom, Wyoming had its first all-woman jury.

When Wyoming became a state in 1890, women's suffrage became part of its constitution. Morris died in 1902, privileged to vote in Wyoming's elections but not for president of the United States.

★ **Wyoming's women won the vote in 1912.**
Library of Congress LC-USZ6-2166

Wyoming also boasted the nation's first woman governor, Nellie Tayloe Ross. Ross became the state's top official in 1924. Her husband the governor had died in office, and Ross won a special election to succeed him. Then Ross went on to a national job. In 1930, she became the first woman to serve as director of the US Mint.

A Glimmer of Hope

WOMEN WHO lived far from the big cities of the East offered a flicker of hope to Susan and Elizabeth in 1869. Men in Wyoming's legislature voted for women's suffrage. Though Wyoming was still a territory and not yet a state, suffragists now had a triumph on which to hang their bonnets.

Two months later, the Utah Territory legislature also enfranchised women, much to the surprise of outsiders. Utah was settled largely by Mormons, known formally as the Church of Jesus Christ of Latter-day Saints. Mormons practiced polygamy, allowing one man to have several wives. Polygamy offended most Americans. Antisuffragists accused Utah's men of trying to build political power by giving their women the vote.

In general, Westerners took a broader view of women's rights than Easterners did. As in colonial times, Western women worked side by side with their husbands on ranches and farms. Little by little, women were permitted to elect school board members and, later, to vote in local elections.

But, as in the East, suffragists ran into roadblocks. In 1877, a hot campaign for women's suffrage in Colorado brought scorn from a Roman Catholic bishop. A Protestant minister preached that suffragists were "bawling, ranting women, bristling for their rights." Though Elizabeth Stanton and Susan Anthony boarded trains and headed west to speak to Coloradans, their efforts failed.

Over the next 13 years, the suffrage movement in Colorado regrouped. Scores of women organized local efforts by making their case through newspapers and political groups. They changed men's minds, one at a time. Time helped, as the Populist political party built support in the West. Made up of farm men—and their wives—Populists believed in votes for women.

Colorado's busy suffragists also had the leadership of a young up-and-comer named Carrie Chapman Catt, an Iowa school principal turned organizer who was sent west to help them. Victory at last came to Colorado's women in 1890, when men voted in a general election to enfranchise women. Idaho followed in 1896.

7

Prisoners in a Gilded Age

D ESPITE SOME success in the West, the campaign for suffrage slowed down in the 1870s and 1880s. Americans' zest for reform after the Civil War began to cool down. The United States entered its Gilded Age, when the men who ran big business—iron, steel, railroads, meatpacking, and oil—launched America into years of growth.

To get that job done, business and industry needed workers for factories and offices.

Companies grew so big the men in charge never met most of their workers face to face. Corporate bosses had no contact with the women and men who ran spoolers in cotton mills or pulled steel from blast furnaces. Companies squeezed out as much work as they could from their employees. Typical workweeks ran 10 to 12 hours a day, every day but Sunday. Often there was no place to sit down, no fresh air, and no time to take a break.

From the beginning, women worked many of the same jobs as men but with far less pay. Until Massachusetts changed its laws in 1874, women and children worked six days a week, just like the men did.

The swell of new immigrants from Eastern Europe, Russia, and Italy offered industry a supply of cheap labor, and immigrant women did their part on production lines. Others scraped out a living doing piecework at home as seamstresses for the garment industry or as cigar makers in overcrowded city tenements that overflowed with people and garbage.

Growing businesses needed clerical workers to staff their offices and hired well-schooled women as copyists to handwrite letters and documents. Once typewriters were invented, women became typists. Companies needed someone to do their paperwork, but a

★ ABOVE: As late as 1917, girls like this 15-year-old worked as typists. Library of Congress LC-USZ62-47377

★ LEFT: Tenement families did piecework at home. In this photo, children ages 10 and 5 help to pick nuts from their shells. The father, laid off from the railroad, refused to do piecework.

Library of Congress LC-DIG-nclc-04143

typist's job was nonetheless considered low-level work.

Whether office workers or shop clerks, most young women left their jobs when they married. As before the Civil War, married women in the growing middle class were expected to live in their domestic sphere, seeing to their husbands' needs and raising their children.

Squeezed into Second Place

SOCIALLY AND politically, life for women in the Gilded Age changed slowly. Victorian ideals still reigned. Though more girls went to school and a lucky few to college, many American girls did not stay in school much past age 10.

Girls didn't play sports or exercise much beyond going for walks. Pale faces were fashionable. Ladies kept their hats and gloves on to keep the sun from their faces and hands, and they practiced good posture, held up in part by corsets lined with steel rods.

Middle- and upper-class women were wrapped up in undergarments and fashions that made them prisoners in their own clothes. Even hardworking farm women, as well as immigrants who worked as servants and factory workers, had to put up with long, heavy dresses.

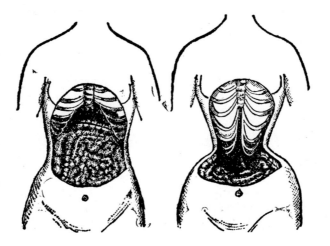

★ ABOVE: "Sensible mothers" wore corsets, as did their children—or so this ad claimed.

★ LEFT: An image from 1903 shows a woman's internal organs in their natural space (*left*) and squeezed by a corset (*right*).

Library of Congress LC-DIG-ppmsca-02907

How Comfortable Is a Corset?

FASHIONS in the 1800s dictated that women and older girls wear corsets to draw in their waist to tiny proportions.

But how did they feel? You can experiment with a bandage designed to wrap an injured ankle, knee, or elbow. But for this activity, you'll wrap it around your middle.

You'll Need

➤ Tight T-shirt
➤ Leggings or sweatpants
➤ Helper
➤ 1 elastic bandage 4 inches wide (these come in packages with metal clips to fasten them)
➤ Camera

Put on the tight T-shirt and leggings. Ask your helper to wrap the bandage around your middle. Lift your arms. Start by holding the end of the bandage on your chest, as shown. Once your helper has made one wrap, lift your arms away from your body.

Your helper makes more wraps, working down your middle. To create your "waist," each wrap should be tighter and tighter. When your helper has finished wrapping, the wraps should end below your belt line.

Your helper should fasten the end of the bandage to itself using the metal clips.

How do you feel? (At first, this might not feel too uncomfortable.) Ask your helper to take your picture, front and back. You'll be surprised to see how different you look with your waist wrapped.

Now how comfortable do you feel? Are you able to walk and move easily with your waist wrapped?

Carefully loosen the clips and remove the bandage. Now how do you feel? Years ago, women often wore their corsets day *and* night. How did they ever get used to them?

Not only were clothes confining and inconvenient, but the corsets worn underneath were dangerous. Years of wearing tight corsets actually squeezed women's lungs, stomachs, and other organs out of place. If anyone knew that, they wore them anyway. The author Laura Ingalls Wilder wrote about the corsets she had to wear in the early 1880s when she was about 14:

Her corsets were a sad affliction to her, from the time she put them on in the morning until she took them off at night. But when girls pinned up their hair and wore skirts down to their shoetops, they must wear corsets.

"You should wear them all night," Ma said. Mary did, but Laura could not bear at night the torment of the steels that would not let her draw a deep breath. Always before she could get to sleep, she had to take off her corsets.

Susan Anthony Takes the Stand

SUSAN B. Anthony may have disliked Victoria Woodhull, but she agreed with her on one count. Woodhull said that parts of the 14th and 15th Amendments *did* permit women to vote, precisely because their wording did not forbid it. Anthony agreed, and in the election of 1872, she, her sisters, and some friends showed up to vote at the polls in her home of Rochester, New York. That day, no one turned her away, and Anthony, together with 14 women, cast her ballot like every other man at the polling place.

Two weeks later, a lawman knocked on Anthony's door. He arrested her for breaking a federal law by voting in a national election. The following summer, Anthony faced government lawyers in court. From the first, every onlooker knew that matters would go against her. The judge, in fact, wrote his opinion before the trial took place. He refused to allow Anthony to speak in her own defense, and he also instructed the jury—all men—to find her guilty without even a moment to deliberate behind closed doors.

Anthony was convicted and fined $100. She then told the judge, "I will never pay a dollar of your unjust penalty." She went on to say that she would happily pay off the $10,000 debt she owed for publishing the *Revolution*, but she would never pay the $100 fine.

Susan's words cut through the air. She was proud that her magazine had taught "all women to do precisely as I have done, rebel against your man-made, unjust, unconstitutional forms of law, which tax, fine, imprison, and hang women, while denying them the right of representation in the government."

The crafty judge had his surprising answer ready. "Madam," he said to Anthony, "the Court will not order you to stand committed [*to go to jail*] until the fine is paid."

For the moment, the judge had won. Anthony never paid the fine, and no one tried to collect it. By not ordering Anthony to jail, he stopped her from appealing to a higher court of law.

Anthony and Stanton now realized that they would never win votes for women by going through the US court system. The two friends, along with the other suffragists of NWSA, decided that they must persuade

Paint Your Plate!

In the 1800s, girls and women were restricted in their choice of art. It wasn't considered appropriate for women to paint big pictures in oils or to carve large sculptures. Only items that could decorate homes were thought to be ladylike.

Many women who were skilled artists painted china—cups, saucers, plates, and trays. China painting was considered just a "minor" art. Still, many lovely items sit in china cabinets today, handed down from one generation to the next as family treasures.

You can try your hand at china painting too, using modern materials.

You'll Need
➤ Adult helper
➤ Plain white or clear glass plates, cups, and saucers
➤ Pencil
➤ Practice paper
➤ Old newspaper
➤ Ceramic paints (from a craft store)
➤ Foam deli trays
➤ Assorted paintbrushes
➤ Washable marker
➤ Oven
➤ Potholders or oven mitts

To start, wash and dry the pieces you will paint. Use pencil and paper to practice designs until you create some that you like. Cover your work surface with newspaper to keep it clean.

Read the directions on the paint containers. Pour some of each color onto a deli tray. Following the directions, practice painting your designs on the foam surface. Experiment with the brushes to see what effects you can make—thin, thick, smooth, rough. Also practice mixing and blending colors—that's part of the fun. Remember, practice makes perfect!

Are you ready? Use a washable marker to trace your design onto a piece of china. Carefully add the paint. Allow one layer to dry before you add another. If you don't like what you see, don't worry. You can wipe the fresh paint away and start over.

When you are pleased with your work, it's time to set the paint in by heating the china in the oven. An adult should help you with this step.

Read the directions on the paint containers for finishing your piece. Turn on the oven and set it at the correct temperature.

The adult should help you put your piece in the oven. Set the timer. Remove the piece when time's up. Be sure to use oven mitts.

You are now ready to use your piece of painted china. You can decorate vases and pots and other items as well.

Congress to pass a constitutional amendment. In January 1878, a helpful senator introduced a 16th Amendment to the Constitution. Anthony penned its 24 words: "The right of citizens to vote shall not be denied or abridged by the United States or by any State on account of sex."

In 1878 and every year thereafter until 1919, these words were presented to the US Congress. In time, it became known as the Susan B. Anthony Amendment. But by the time it passed through Congress and was ratified by the states, both Susan Anthony and Elizabeth Stanton were long dead.

"The Head of Medusa"

FOR THE moment, the drive for women's suffrage seemed to have run out of steam. Though their hearts stood strong to their task, Elizabeth Cady Stanton and Susan B. Anthony were growing old, as was Lucy Stone. "The cause" was in the doldrums, like a huge ship adrift at sea with no wind to fill its sails.

The outspoken ladies who stood front and center for suffrage represented only a fraction

★ **A pictorial newspaper poked fun at Susan Anthony after she was convicted in a US court for voting.** Library of Congress LC-USZ62-114833

THE DAILY GRAPHIC

AN ILLUSTRATED EVENING NEWSPAPER.

39 & 41 PARK PLACE.

VOL. I—NO. 81.   NEW YORK, THURSDAY, JUNE 5, 1873.   FIVE CENTS.

GRAPHIC STATUES, NO. 17.—"THE WOMAN WHO DARED."

of American women. Many homemakers stood in the mainstream with other Americans. The plain truth was that most middle-class women didn't care much about having the right to vote.

True enough, more girls and young women were going to high school and college. But once they married, most middle-class women were content to work at home and raise their families. They did not cross the invisible line that separated them from the world of men. By tradition, America's "true women" were taught to believe that they were responsible for keeping the nation's morals in good shape. In "polite" society, women were believed to be purer than men.

Ministers in pulpits and politicians in government agreed that America's women must stay pure and untouched by the world beyond their doors. They saw no need for women to take part in public life. Their husbands were there to shield them from the corruption on American streets and in American business.

And yet, when some homemakers found their very way of life at risk, they began to change their views about getting into politics.

The threat was alcohol. Strong drink—rum, whiskey, and bourbon—ruined the lives of many. Drunkenness was an issue across America. All too often, men who went on drinking binges came home to beat their wives and children. Fathers and husbands ended up fired from their jobs.

As keepers of their homes and families, women didn't have jobs to bring in money, or any way to hire lawyers to protect themselves. That left many women and children hungry and often homeless.

A lot of these luckless women had grown up believing what they heard in church: that God's plan for the world was for men to have power over their wives and children. But the Bible didn't offer a clear solution for women whose husbands were sickened by alcohol. Some women were devoted churchgoers, and they prayed for God's guidance as they looked into their own souls for answers. There they found them—they broke with church tradition and decided to step into the public sphere to call for prohibition and ban alcoholic drinks across the nation.

Ordinary housewives began to speak in public and petition their town and state governments. For a time, prohibitionist women won some victories. Yet when they spoke in public, men jeered and catcalled.

One minister called these women "a monstrosity of nature, a subverter [*threat*] of society, the cave of despair, the head of Medusa." To this man of God, a woman who spoke in public was as frightful as a monster in a Greek myth with snakes for hair.

★ "Poverty, Misery, Crime, Death"—"King Alcohol" ruined lives in many American families.

Like women who had spoken out against slavery 40 years earlier, female prohibitionists found they had no true voice. All too often, the daily grind of local politics took place in beer-soaked saloons where no "nice" woman with good morals was welcome.

Frances Willard led the charge for prohibition as leader of the Woman's Christian Temperance Union. Willard understood that winning prohibition was a political issue as well as a moral one. In her eyes, women were keepers of America's virtue, but it was no good keeping women behind closed doors.

Willard agreed that women must have the vote. By linking prohibition with suffrage, she cracked open the door to new ideas.

For the first time, American women who hadn't thought much about winning the vote began to change their minds. Into their white ribbons that stood for purity, they twisted the yellow ribbons of suffragists. As the 1870s and 1880s rolled on, many mainstream American women joined the suffrage movement.

Willard's push for the vote had both pluses and minuses. For one, suffragists now had more members to back them and more money at hand. But when Willard linked prohibition with winning the vote, women's suffrage gained even more enemies. As always, powerful men in the liquor business had no intention of closing saloons and banning alcohol.

Going Clubbing

As AMERICAN life prospered, middle-class women began to have fewer children, which freed them to spend time away from home. A few free hours during the week allowed women to socialize at their churches and join clubs in their communities. Gardening clubs, library societies and book clubs, missionary and prohibition groups—in big cities and small towns—welcomed women to share their interests.

In parlors at homes across America, millions of women began to find a voice in their

★ Frances Willard.
Library of Congress LC-USZ61-790

★ *Puck* magazine made fun of women's clubs. This cartoon compares a women's club with men's clubs that were popular in the late 1800s. Library of Congress LC-USZC2-1021

communities. Many women were eager to stretch their minds and learn new things. Women read up on topics and then wrote long reports to deliver at business meetings. They read and reported on all kinds of subjects from music to missions to Greek literature to important political and social issues, suffrage among them.

Most women's clubs, including many church groups, stayed independent of men's influence. Women thought of their clubs as part of their sphere and proudly raised money and ran their budgets independent of their husbands.

Club women typically put on an appearance as "do-gooders" in their cities and towns. They raised money for orphanages and sewed clothes for the poor. By masking their work as charity, they kept men from interfering with their chance to simply enjoy using their minds.

Whatever their interests, club women had one thing in common: they took time from discussing business to socialize over cups of tea and plates of cake and cookies. "Ladies, we must eat and drink something together or we shall never get acquainted with each other," proclaimed Julia Ward Howe, who besides being a suffragist prized her friendships with women in her clubs.

Women joined clubs according to their interests, but their clubs also mirrored American life. Protestant, Mormon, and Jewish

★ "American Woman and Her Political Peers." In 1893, Henrietta Briggs-Wall designed this image of Frances Willard surrounded by others not allowed to vote. They are a mentally disabled man, a criminal, an American Indian, and a madman.

Kansas State Historical Society

women had their own clubs, as did working-class women and newly arrived immigrants. Other groups of Catholic and Southern Baptist women joined clubs but did not enjoy the same independence from the men who ruled their churches. In any case, women rarely socialized with members of other faiths. Protestants spent time with Protestants, Catholics with Catholics, and Jews with Jews.

A Matter of Race

WOMEN'S CLUBS also divided themselves by race along the color line. In the 1800s and long into the 1900s, race divided the United States. In the South, state governments made laws that forced black Americans to live apart from whites. These laws, known as Jim Crow laws, established segregation as a way of life.

In the North, Americans also divided themselves by race. Though Jim Crow laws did not officially segregate blacks and whites, an invisible wall separated the races. Blacks and whites worshipped in separate churches, got their hair cut in separate barbershops, attended different parties, and mostly attended separate schools.

Most middle-class whites viewed all blacks as ignorant and inferior, even those who were well educated and worked as doctors, lawyers, and teachers. Middle-class blacks had to

Design a Suffragist Postcard

SUFFRAGE postcards used humor to make their point.

What do you have to say about our world? Is something going on that *you* want to change? Perhaps you'd like a better playground where you live. Maybe there's a need for your town to have a community garden or a place where people can play checkers and chess. What about bike trails?

Put your idea on a postcard, add a stamp, and mail it. Be sure to make your postcard from sturdy cardboard, or buy a plain postcard at the post office. Your postcard must be:

★ This postcard appeared in 1906, well before women won the vote.

➤ Rectangular
➤ At least 3½ inches high by 5 inches long by 0.007 inch thick
➤ No more than 4¼ inches high by 6 inches long by 0.016 inch thick

There are many ways to express your thoughts. Here are a few suggestions:

➤ Draw a cartoon.
➤ Take a picture, print it out, and glue it to your card.
➤ Make a collage with bits of colored cloth or tissue paper and watered-down glue.
➤ Write in cursive, glue along the lines, and top with string or yarn.

On the back, write your message on the left side, as shown. Be polite, and say thank you. Address the card and add a stamp. Be sure to research exactly who should receive your postcard.

Note: If you decorate your postcard, have it weighed at the post office before you mail it.

constantly prove their worth to whites. In late 1800s America, whites and people of color did not socialize.

Black women faced a double struggle: to achieve their rights as people of color and also to combat their second-class roles as women. Like white women, black women banded together in the late 1800s to form church groups and clubs. These like-minded women shared the same plans to provide better schools, good jobs, and other reforms to improve life in black communities.

In 1896, a number of influential women's groups banded together to form the National Association of Colored Women (NACW). As their motto they chose inspiring words: "Lifting as We Climb." Several influential suffragists joined them. They included the scholar

★ **ABOVE:** These young women were officers of the Women's League of Newport, Rhode Island. This club for black women worked to improve the community. Library of Congress LC-USZ62-51555

★ **LEFT:** Children and a caregiver stand on the steps of the Women's Newport League House, a day **nursery.** Library of Congress LC-USZ62-51556

Mary Church Terrell, journalist Ida B. Wells-Barnett, and Harriet Tubman, now 74 years old and a living legend.

When it came to votes for women, NACW members were more vocal than white club members. Black women were sure that hav-

Mary Church Terrell

Mary Church Terrell was born in Memphis, Tennessee, during the Civil War to parents who had once been enslaved. Her father became a successful businessman in segregated Memphis. He realized that his daughter could not get the education she deserved at home and sent Mary north to Ohio to go to school.

Like Lucy Stone before her, Terrell attended Oberlin College, as always welcoming to both women and people of color. Graceful and smart, she studied classics at college and learned to read and write French, German, and Italian. She put her flair for languages to use throughout her life, especially when she represented black women at a meeting in Germany in 1904. Terrell became the talk of the conference when she presented her views in three languages, the only delegate with such talent.

Terrell's far-ranging interests marked her as a strong progressive. She served as the first president of the National Association of Colored Women and later helped to found the National Association for the Advancement of Colored People (NAACP). She also taught in schoolrooms and colleges and became the first black woman to serve on a school board in Washington, DC. She and her husband, a lawyer who rose to become a judge, welcomed two daughters into their family.

Terrell's gift for speaking made her a popular figure at lectures and conferences. She pushed her views about the dignity of black women and equality for all people wherever she went. At the age of 89 in 1952, Terrell hobbled into a whites-only cafeteria in a dime store, leaning on her cane. No one would serve her a meal. Still, she had made her point.

★ **Mary Church Terrell.**
Library of Congress LC-USZ62-54722

But times were changing. Months later, the manager of the same cafeteria invited her back for a visit, where he treated her to coffee and a piece of pie.

A Bible for Women

Elizabeth Cady Stanton hated to hear ministers preach that women were evil. Their views, she claimed, shamed women.

When our bishops, archbishops and ordained clergymen stand up in their pulpits ... with reverential voice, they make the women of their congregation believe that there really is some divine authority for their subjection.

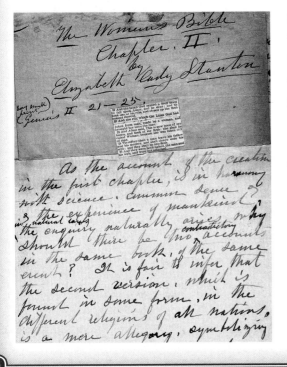

★ **A manuscript page of the *Woman's Bible* penned by Elizabeth Cady Stanton.** Library of Congress

In 1895, Stanton and others published the *Woman's Bible*. They hoped to correct mistakes in people's thinking. They pointed out that parts of the Bible said different things.

For example, one passage said that God created Eve, the first woman, from Adam's rib—which made her second in God's eyes. However, Stanton noted, in the very first creation story, God created Adam and Eve at the same time—as equals.

The *Woman's Bible* also challenged another belief. In his Letter to the Corinthians, the apostle Paul wrote that women "should be quiet in church." Churchmen used this verse to stop women from serving as ministers or priests.

But as reformers pointed out, the very same Paul also wrote, "There can be neither Jew nor Greek, slave nor free, male nor female." Common sense said that the Bible's words must be open to new ways of understanding.

Susan Anthony was dismayed when Stanton published the *Woman's Bible*. Anthony welcomed women of all faiths, as well as nonbelievers. She did not want the *Woman's Bible* to draw fire on the suffrage movement.

Young suffragists feared that Stanton's far-reaching views would make them outcasts. They voted to censure—formally criticize—Stanton at their annual meeting. Anthony could not stop them.

From then on, Stanton pulled away from the suffrage movement. She continued to write and publish her freethinking ideas, and she never regretted them. But as the suffrage movement pressed on, Stanton was nearly forgotten.

In the 1920s, when a new generation of women recorded the history of women's suffrage, Elizabeth Cady Stanton was "written out" of the story. The authors idolized Anthony, and they lied about some of her deeds in order to build up her name. These writers claimed that Anthony had attended the first women's rights convention in Seneca Falls in 1848. That was not true, and they knew it. Several decades passed before students of the women's rights movement gave Elizabeth Cady Stanton her rightful place in history.

ing the vote would help them change society. In 1912, NACW went on record to support women's suffrage. Their white counterpart, the General Federation of Woman's Clubs, did not endorse women's suffrage until 1914.

Writing Their Story

In July 1876, Americans celebrated the 100th anniversary, the Centennial, of the Declaration of Independence. To Elizabeth Stanton and Susan Anthony, however, it seemed there was little to celebrate because women still had no right to vote. Together with their loyal friend Matilda Joslyn Gage, they rewrote their *Declaration of Rights for Women*, and Anthony asked to present it at the official celebration in Philadelphia. She was told no. There weren't any seats, claimed the men in charge.

On July 4, 1876, Anthony and four friends finagled their way into the giant convention hall. As the Declaration of Independence was read aloud, the five women rose from their chairs and headed toward the stage. Anthony handed a parchment copy of the women's

★ **Uninvited, Susan B. Anthony and others passed out copies of this document to men celebrating the 100th anniversary of the Declaration of Independence.** Library of Congress rbpe 16000300

DECLARATION AND PROTEST

OF THE

WOMEN OF THE UNITED STATES

BY THE

NATIONAL WOMAN SUFFRAGE ASSOCIATION,

JULY 4th, 1876.

WHILE the Nation is buoyant with patriotism, and all hearts are attuned to praise, it is with sorrow we come to strike the one discordant note, on this hundredth anniversary of our country's birth. When subjects of Kings, Emperors, and Czars, from the Old World, join in our National Jubilee, shall the women of the Republic refuse to lay their hands with benedictions on the nation's head? Surveying America's Exposition, surpassing in magnificence those of London, Paris, and Vienna, shall we not rejoice at the success of the youngest rival among the nations of the earth? May not our hearts, in unison with all, swell with pride at our great achievements as a people; our free speech, free press, free schools, free church, and the rapid progress we have made in material wealth, trade, commerce, and the inventive arts? And we do rejoice, in the success thus far, of our experiment of self-government. Our faith is firm and unwavering in the broad principles of human rights, proclaimed in 1776, not only as abstract truths, but as the corner stones of a republic. Yet, we cannot forget, even in this glad hour, that while all men of every race, and clime, and condition, have been invested with the full rights of citizenship, under our hospitable flag, all women still suffer the degradation of disfranchisement.

Our history, the past hundred years, has been a series of assumptions and usurpations of power over woman, in direct opposition to the principles of just government, acknowledged by the United States at its foundation, which are:

First. The natural rights of each individual to self-government.

Second. The exact equality of these rights.

Third. That these rights, when not delegated by the individual, are retained by the individual.

Fourth. That no person can exercise the rights of others without delegated authority.

Fifth. That the non-use of these rights does not destroy them.

And for the violation of these fundamental principles of our Government, we arraign our rulers on this 4th day of July, 1876,—and these are our

ARTICLES OF IMPEACHMENT.

BILLS OF ATTAINDER have been passed by the introduction of the word "male" into all the State constitutions, denying to woman the right of suffrage, and thereby making sex a crime—an exercise of power clearly forbidden in Article 1st, Sections 9th and 10th of the United States Constitution.

Jump in Time to a Suffrage Rhyme

DID you ever hear this nursery rhyme?

Miss Lulu had a baby, she called him tiny Tim.
She put him in the bathtub, to see if he could swim.
He drank up all the water! He ate up all the soap!
He tried to swallow the bathtub, but it wouldn't go down his throat!
Call for the doctor!
Call for the nurse!
Call for the lady with the alligator purse!
"Mumps!" said the doctor. "Measles!" said the nurse.
"Vote!" said the lady with the alligator purse!

Volunteers at the Susan B. Anthony House in Rochester, New York, will tell you that the "lady with the alligator purse" was none other than Anthony herself. Her purse, actu-ally a roomy handled bag made of alligator skin, went with her everywhere. In the 1890s, Anthony spent several months in California helping its women work for suffrage. Anthony went home without success in California, but her alligator purse left an impression. Children picked up on Anthony's fame and added it—and her handbag—to their jump-rope rhyme.

Get some exercise as you chant this enchanting rhyme.

You'll Need
➤ Jump rope
➤ A roomy spot

Practice saying the rhyme until you have it memorized. Think about how it will fit the rhythm of jumping rope—especially line 4. When you are ready, grab your rope and go outside. Have fun jumping. Can you imagine Susan Anthony jumping rope when she was young?

★ Susan B. Anthony House, Inc.

declaration to none other than the acting vice president of the United States, Thomas Ferry. The other women handed out copies to men in the audience.

With that task done, Anthony went outside and climbed onto a bandstand in the humid July day. Her friend Matilda Gage held an umbrella to protect the black-clad Anthony from the sun. People gawked at the 56-year-old woman, dressed in black, who spoke powerful words:

And now, at the close of a hundred years, as the hour-hand of the great clock that marks the centuries point to 1876, we declare our faith in the principle of self-government, our full equality with man in natural rights; that woman was made first for her own happiness, with the absolute right to herself.

A Book for the Ages

As THE nation marked its centennial, Elizabeth Cady Stanton and Susan B. Anthony took stock of their own drive for independence. Anthony was 56; Stanton, nearly 61. In their day, they were thought of as old women. It was time to get their story down on paper.

Working as a team, Stanton and Anthony began to write *A History of Woman Suffrage*. As Anthony wisely pointed out, men had been busy writing their history for centuries, and it was high time for women to do the same. Over the course of several years—well into the 1880s—Stanton and Anthony, sometimes assisted by Matilda Gage, wrote three enormous volumes. Eventually *A History of Woman Suffrage* grew into six books stuffed with details about women's struggle to win the vote—but they were finished long after Stanton and Anthony had died.

Often the friends would disagree as much as they agreed about what to write. Sometimes their writing sessions morphed into arguments, and Anthony would leave Stanton's house to take a walk and give them both time to cool off.

Their disagreements mirrored the differences in their thinking. Anthony, growing older but still filled with fire, fixated on suffrage only; she was sure that once women had the vote they could make America a better place.

Stanton's views grew ever broader. To Stanton, having the right to vote was not enough, only "a crumb" and not a whole loaf. Stanton wanted girls and women to have options in their lives—in their education, their choice of a trade or profession, and their family lives

(whether to use birth control to manage the size of their families).

Elizabeth Cady Stanton had one more radical idea. She wanted society to agree that, in God's eyes, women stood equal with men.

★ Though they often argued about the best way to win rights for women, Susan B. Anthony and Elizabeth Cady Stanton stayed friends for life.

8

Rolling into a New Century

ELIZABETH CADY Stanton wanted to add Lucy Stone's contributions to the book she was writing with Susan B. Anthony. Stanton wrote Stone asking for her help, but Stone wrote back to say no. Their differences were too many, the divide between them too deep.

Thus, at first, Lucy Stone's story and the history of the American Woman Suffrage Association was left out of *A History of Woman Suffrage*. As the months moved on, Elizabeth Stanton and Lucy Stone did not solve their disagreements.

Like young women everywhere, Harriot Stanton Blatch and Alice Stone Blackwell viewed their mothers' quarrels as ancient history. By the late 1880s, they were adults with minds of their own, and they wanted to heal the rift in the suffrage movement.

★ OPPOSITE: At the turn of the 20th century, American women stepped more and more into public life. This illustration depicts the different roles they took on.
Library of Congress LC-DIG-ppmsca-25811

Blatch came to her mother and Susan Anthony with a suggestion for their history book. Blatch believed that Lucy Stone's work needed a place, and she offered to write the missing chapter about Stone and AWSA.

Anthony never warmed to the idea, but Blatch wrote it anyway. Blatch's mother, Elizabeth Cady Stanton, made sure that Anthony paid Blatch for her contribution.

Alice Stone Blackwell was no fan of Susan Anthony, but she also felt that it was time for both sides to come together. She and her father, Henry, nudged their friends toward reuniting with their enemies. Time was marching on, and Lucy Stone agreed that the stories of old battles between suffragists didn't matter to younger women.

Reunited for Reform

In 1890, America's suffragists reunited as the National American Woman Suffrage Association. Once not on speaking terms, Stanton, Anthony, and Stone regrouped as leaders of their party. But the relationship among them was never easy. It was up to the next generation to take up the cause of women's suffrage and work together.

Lucy Stone's health had started to fail, and in 1893, she died. Her lovely voice, so long a force for women's suffrage, was stilled. Stone, who had refused to take her husband's name so long ago, pioneered another change at her death. She was the first person in Massachusetts to ask that her body be cremated instead of buried.

Henry granted her wish, and Stone's ashes were buried in a cemetery without a gravestone. But her voice survives in the thousands of letters she wrote to Henry, Alice, and scores of others. When she died, she left her orders with Alice in her final words: "Make the world better."

★ **Lucy Stone was honored with a stamp by the US Post Office in 1968.**

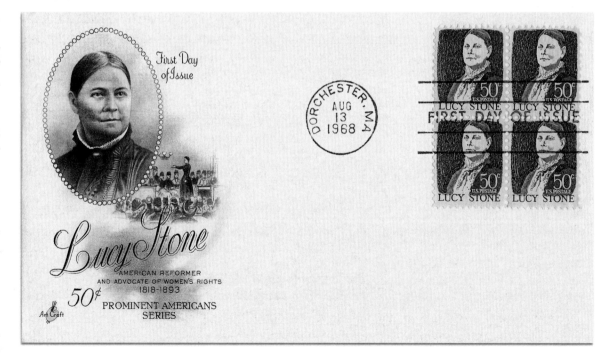

Make Water-Lily Eggs

IN order to raise money, suffragists in Boston turned to a tried-and-true fundraiser—they wrote a cookbook. As busy as they were, suffragists still had families to feed.

The *Woman Suffrage Cook Book*, published in 1886, offered recipes from appetizers to desserts, as well as a section on cooking and personal care for the sick. Some famous names appear—Lucy Stone, Alice Stone Blackwell, Dr. Anna Howard Shaw—as well as ministers and everyday women who proudly called themselves suffragists.

Alice Stone Blackwell's recipe for Water-Lily Eggs sounds much like a recipe that appeared in the 1900s for Eggs à la Goldenrod. An older person in your family might remember them as a special treat.

You can enjoy Alice's delicious offering for breakfast—or anytime! Read Alice's original recipe, and then try the updated one.

ALICE STONE BLACKWELL'S WATER-LILY EGGS

Boil two eggs twenty minutes. Separate whites from yolks. Put on a plate one teaspoonful of flour, a piece of butter the size of a hickory nut, and pepper and salt to taste. On this plate cut up the whites of the eggs into small cubes the size of dice, mixing with flour, salt, etc. Have four tablespoonfuls of milk boiling in a sauce-pan; put the whites in, and let them cook slowly while you make two slices of toast. Spread whites (when flour is thoroughly cooked) over toast. Break the yolks up slightly and salt them, and force through fine strainer over the whites on top of the toast. Holes in strainer should not be larger than pinheads. Serve hot, at once. A very pretty dish, and convenient in case of unexpected company, as bread and eggs are almost always in the house.
—ALICE STONE BLACKWELL.

UPDATED WATER-LILY EGGS

You'll Need

➤ Adult helper
➤ 2 eggs
➤ Small saucepan
➤ Water
➤ Large spoon
➤ Strainer
➤ Salt
➤ Plate
➤ Small paring knife

➤ 1 teaspoon white flour
➤ 2 tablespoons butter
➤ Small glass dish
➤ Salt and pepper to taste
➤ ¼ cup milk
➤ Fork
➤ 2 slices bread
➤ Butter
➤ Toaster or toaster oven

To boil the eggs, place them in a small saucepan and cover with water. Bring the eggs to a boil, turn down the heat, and simmer for 20 minutes. Remove the hard-boiled eggs carefully with a large spoon. Run cold water over them until you can handle them, but they should still be warm.

Peel the eggs and separate the yolks from the whites. Using the back of the spoon, force the yolks through the strainer onto a small dish. Sprinkle with a bit of salt and set aside.

To make the sauce: On the plate, chop up the egg whites and mix with the flour and butter. Sprinkle lightly with salt and pepper. Pour the milk into a small glass dish and stir in the egg-white mixture. Microwave on high power for 30 seconds. Remove and stir a bit with a small fork. Return mixture to microwave and cook again for 15 more seconds. Repeat the process until your mixture is thick and creamy.

While you are cooking the egg-white sauce, toast two slices of bread, but leave them in the toaster. (Hint: If you make toast in a toaster oven, put your breakfast plate on top to warm it. A warm plate means a warmer breakfast!)

When the egg-white sauce is ready, assemble your water lily. Butter the toast and place on a warm plate. Pour the sauce over the toast and sprinkle with the egg yolks.

As Alice Stone Blackwell said, enjoy this "pretty dish"!

Looking Toward a New Century

THE SHINE on the Gilded Age began to tarnish. As the United States moved into the 1890s, the economy lagged. Farmers complained they couldn't get fair prices for their crops because railroads overcharged them for shipping. In cities, immigrants and other poor people were packed into tenement slums and worked long hours for low pay. "Big business" seemed to rule hand in hand with corrupt legislators in city and state governments. It seemed that the rich were getting richer as working people struggled to make a living.

In 1893, trouble came to America's railway system, which had overbuilt and overinvested in the nation's railroads. One company failed, and a "run" on banks—when Americans rushed to turn their bank deposits into cash—followed. Like a house of cards, the system began to teeter; then it collapsed. The depression that followed was the worst that any American had ever seen. About one out of every six workers was left without a job.

Misery fell on big cities where immigrants lived. Packed into tenements with few laws to protect them, these foreign-born workers—men, women, and children—could not improve their lives. Other Americans, forgetting that their own ancestors had also immigrated, looked down on these newcomers.

They made fun of their clothes, their languages, and their religions. Most immigrants coming from Italy were Roman Catholic; others arriving from Poland and Russia were Jews.

A Woman for Change

BY 1890, the situation in America's slums was turning desperate. Yet some Americans strived to make better lives for others. The best-known reformer was a woman, Jane Addams, whose work with poor immigrants in Chicago sparked a national movement.

Like many women who graduated from college in the Gilded Age, Addams became a well-educated lady without a job. She drifted from one thing to the next, studying medicine for a time but always returning home to her family. They were perfectly content to have her there.

When Addams was 27, she and her lifelong friend Ellen Starr sailed to England. A chance visit to a settlement house in the slums of London transformed her life. There, at Toynbee Hall, upper-class people and poor Londoners could come together to work for social reform.

With one look at Toynbee Hall, Addams knew she had found her life's calling. In 1890, she and Starr bought an old mansion that had belonged to a wealthy Chicagoan, and

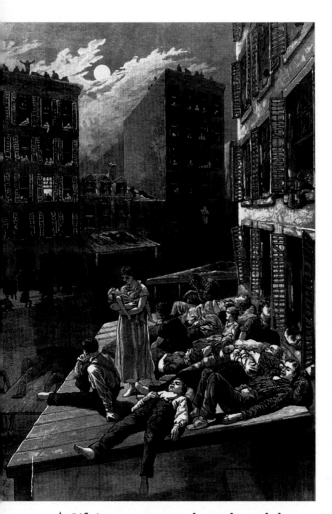

★ **Life in tenements was hot and crowded, as this 1882 illustration showed.** Library of Congress

they named it Hull House in his honor. They moved in and opened their doors to their immigrant neighbors. Addams recruited other college women to help her, and within a year 2,000 poor people came to Hull House to enrich their lives. America's Settlement Movement was born.

Addams welcomed everyone into her rambling home. Hull House sat in Chicago's 19th Ward, whose population reflected the mix of people in American cities—"Americans, Belgians, Bohemians, Canadians, Danes, English, French, Germans, Greeks, Hollanders, Hungarians, Irish, Italians, Lithuanians, Mexicans, Norwegians, Poles, Russians, Scots, Spaniards, Swedes, Swiss, Welsh, Negroes, Chinese, and divers [*diverse*] odds and ends."

Addams ran a kindergarten, kids' clubs, and night school for adults. She taught cooking and home health care. Hull House offered a library, swimming pool, drama club, and job center. All the while, Addams stormed rich

★ **Jane Addams.** Library of Congress LC-B2-107-6

★ **For more than 100 years, little girls worked in textile mills.** Library of Congress LC-USZ62-18108

Matilda Joslyn Gage

Thousands of women contributed to the push for women's suffrage, and their names appear in letters, newspaper articles, and books. Most were not household names like Elizabeth Cady Stanton, Lucy Stone, or Susan B. Anthony.

Matilda Joslyn Gage was one of these unsung heroines. Gage worked with Anthony and Stanton to update Stanton's *Declaration of Rights for Women* from her 1848 version to an updated version in 1876. A gifted writer like Stanton, Gage also worked on the early volumes of *A History of Woman Suffrage*.

Stanton admired Gage's knack for "rummaging through old libraries" in search of hidden stories about women's lives. Gage believed that male writers had willfully cut women's contributions out of the pages of history. It was a woman, Catherine Littlefield Greene, who invented the cotton gin, Gage wrote, not Eli Whitney.

Gage had an unusual friendship with Native American women of the Mohawk nation and was a member of their Wolf Clan. Gage's own "rummaging" and research led her to write a series of articles that pointed out that women of the Iroquois nation lived nearly as social equals to men. Women bought and sold their own property, and they were entitled to keep their children if they divorced their husbands.

Gage's children grew up with independent minds. When her daughter Maud dropped out of law school to marry an author, Gage was dismayed. Still, she moved into her daughter and son-in-law's home, where they had spirited talks about American life. The young man's name was L. Frank Baum, and in a 14-book series for young people, he created a magic land where women were equal to men and everyone was ruled by a wise witch. He titled his first book *The Wizard of Oz*.

Like her ally Elizabeth Cady Stanton, Gage held radical views about organized religion and had harsh words for church teachings that kept women under the rule of men. Her outspoken personality made her enemies among other suffragists who feared that her bold ideas would threaten their work. As with Stanton, Matilda Joslyn Gage was "written out" of suffrage history until the 1990s, when scholars brought her work to light.

★ **This cartoon points out that Iroquois women, considered "savages," had rights denied to other women. The suffragist carrying a staff is probably Matilda Joslyn Gage.** Library of Congress LC-USZC2-1189

WE, THE WOMEN OF THE IROQUOIS:
Own the land, the lodge, the children.
Ours is the right of adoption, of life or death;
Ours the right to raise up and depose chiefs;
Ours the right of representation at all councils;
Ours the right to make and abrogate treaties;
Ours the supervision over domestic and foreign policies;
Ours the trusteeship of the tribal property;
Our lives are valued again as high as man's.

Chicagoans, pleading for them to provide the money she needed to help her visitors.

While Addams operated Hull House, a series of energetic, creative women walked through her door. Susan Anthony came calling, as did women who backed labor reform. Addams became a suffragist and a friend of "working girls," working-class women who labored in factories and sweatshops.

As time went on, Addams became convinced that social reform was her true vocation. She got involved in everything from Chicago's schools and garbage collection to fighting the sordid business in illegal drugs. Then she went national.

As a reformer, Addams became the foremost example of a suffragist working at a job. She had goals to reach, both for Hull House and for America itself. To meet her aims, she needed the right to vote. How else was she to have a voice in the halls of government?

New Woman, No Vote

As the 1890s wore on, Susan B. Anthony and Elizabeth Cady Stanton, now in their 70s, could not keep up with the physical demands of travel and meeting the public. But there were promising candidates to step up as suffrage leaders.

First, Anthony tapped Carrie Chapman Catt. Catt made a name for herself in Iowa's prairie towns helping women to win the vote. Before they married, she and her husband agreed that Catt would have four months every year to travel and campaign for the women's vote. George Catt stood firm in his stand for women's rights and took pride in his wife's work.

George Catt became ill not long after Carrie Catt took over as NAWSA's leader in 1900. She returned to his side to care for him, and Anna Howard Shaw stepped up as the association's new president.

Shaw, both a doctor and a minister, electrified audiences with her powerful speeches. However, Shaw lacked the same gift for organizing suffragists that sparked the careers of Susan B. Anthony and Carrie Chapman Catt. Like a slow-moving train, "the cause" never stopped but for a time chugged uphill, seeming to be running out of steam.

As the new generation took over, the founders faded away. In 1902, Elizabeth Cady Stanton died in her daughter's home. Harriot Stanton Blatch told the tale of her mother's final hours. Stanton insisted on rising from her bed and got dressed. Grasping a table, she acted as though she faced an audience and began to make a speech, her lips moving in silence. Not long thereafter, she died.

★ **Carrie Chapman Catt worked for reform all her life.** Library of Congress LC-USZ62-110995

★ **Unlike their Victorian mothers, New Women enjoyed sports like swimming, tennis, and cycling.** Library of Congress LC-USZ62-83510

Four years later, Susan B. Anthony faced her own death at her home in Rochester, New York. Sickened by a series of strokes and a failing heart, Anthony spent her last days in bed, surrounded by her sister suffragists. As the end drew near, she mouthed the names of scores of people who had touched her life over 81 years. "Failure is impossible," she murmured, her last words that made sense. Then she, too, was gone. It was 1906.

Lucy Stone, Elizabeth Cady Stanton, and Susan B. Anthony had worked their entire lives to win the vote for America's women. Not one of them lived long enough to see her life's work made a reality.

Anthony had tried to leave the suffrage movement in good hands, but it faltered. The grassroots push to win votes for women state by state was stuck. More than 10 years had passed since Carrie Chapman Catt had succeeded in getting men in Colorado to give its women the right to vote. When suffragists came together, their meetings looked like a minister "preaching to the choir." Suffragists attracted only other suffragists who thought the same way they did.

Many people asked whether women needed the vote at all. Life was moving on, and women's lives had begun to change. By 1900, Americans had become accustomed to seeing the New Woman, as she was called, at work in offices and shops. Women were welcomed in college classes and showed up as doctors, ministers, and teachers. Like men, women were free to enjoy the nation's hot new mode of transportation: bicycling. A new twist on bloomers, bicycle suits freed them to "wheel" in comfort.

By all appearances, this New Woman had a rewarding life. She was educated and had money in her pocket. Americans idealized her as an example of womanly virtue to overcome the dark morals of money-grubbing men.

Americans prized the accomplishments of women like Frances Willard and Jane Addams who used their influence to make America a better place. They looked to both reformers as examples of perfect womanhood, who stood far above the grime of street politics and smoky saloons. Why should these perfect women dirty their hands with politics?

Willard and Addams did not agree. They were perfectly happy to win the vote—even if their hands got dirty in the process.

Sisterly Suffrage

THESE WERE new days for women at the bottom of the social ladder as well. Men who organized labor unions had little regard for women who worked in factories. Most believed that working women took jobs away

Sing a Song of Suffragists

IN the late 1800s, suffragists built up their spirits at their meetings by singing. There are many copies of suffrage songbooks tucked away in family attics and libraries. Songs about women's suffrage also appeared as popular sheet music in the 1900s and were sung by popular artists of the day.

Build your spirit for women's suffrage. Here are three songs you will recognize with no problem. They are sung to tunes you should already know!

DARE YOU DO IT?

Sung to the tune of "The Battle Hymn of the Republic"

There's a wave of indignation
Rolling 'round and 'round the
    land,
And its meaning is so mighty
And its mission is so grand,
That none but knaves and
    cowards
Dare deny its just demand,
As we go marching on.

Chorus

Men and brothers, dare you
    do it?
Men and brothers, dare you
    do it?
Men and brothers, dare you
    do it,
As we go marching on?
Ye men who wrong your
    mothers,
And your wives and sisters, too,
How dare you rob companions
Who are always brave and true?
How dare you make them
    servants
Who are all the world to you,
As they go marching on?

Chorus repeats

Whence came your foolish
    notion

Now so greatly overgrown,
That a woman's sober judgment
Is not equal to your own?
Has God ordained that suffrage
Is a gift to you alone,
While life goes marching on?

Chorus repeats

THREE BLIND MEN

Sung to the tune of "Three Blind Mice"

Three blind men,
Three blind men,
See how they stare,
See how they stare;
They each ran off with a wom-
    an's right.
And they each went blind in a
    single night.
Did you ever behold such a
    gruesome sight
As these blind men?
Three blind men,
Three blind men,—
The man who won't,
The man who can't,
And then the coward who
    dares not try;
They're not fit to live and not fit
    to die.
Did you ever see such a three-
    cornered lie
As these blind men?

WOMAN

Sung to the tune of "America"

O woman, 'tis of thee,
Hope of humanity,
Of thee we sing.
Mother of all the race,
Affection's dwelling-place,
For thy sweet love and grace
Our plaudits ring.
No name like thy dear name,
No fame like thy fair fame,
Thy name we love;
Through all our toilsome days,
Through all our devious ways,
Be thine our grateful praise,
All praise above.
Let anguish pass away,
Let rapture reign today,
Let grace abound.
In strains of joy and mirth,
Let all the sons of earth
Proclaim thy matchless worth,
The world around.
Equal of all the race,
Take now thy rightful place
By land and sea;
We'll scorn the tyrants' lust,
And pledge our faith and trust
To evermore be just
And true to thee.

Stump speaking—

In the days of "Old Dobbin" and Derby hats Mrs. Harriet Stanton Blatch exhorted the Wall Street crowds.

★ Like her mother, Elizabeth Cady Stanton, Harriot Stanton Blatch hoped to change men's minds about votes for women. Library of Congress

LC-USZ62-7097

★ LEFT: A cartoonist took a bitter view of the ruins of the Triangle Shirtwaist Company. The sign on the building reads "Girls Wanted." Library of Congress LC-USZC4-5712

★ ABOVE: With escape doors locked and no way out, 146 workers died in the Triangle Shirtwaist fire.

Library of Congress LC-DIG-ppmsca-05641

from men—and that having women in the workforce lowered pay for everyone.

By 1900, working women had begun to find a voice, and several women-only labor unions had formed. Among their biggest fans was Elizabeth Stanton's daughter Harriot Blatch, who was building upon her mother's work.

Elizabeth Cady Stanton had prized the right of the individual educated woman to vote. Blatch, who lived in England and witnessed the rise of labor unions for working people, had different ideas. In keeping with her times, Blatch believed that women of all classes, from social elites to working-class laborers, should join together to push for suffrage. Blatch lived and breathed the fresh air of the Progressive Movement.

Progressivism was taking hold in the United States. Progressives found their voices during the depression of the 1890s, when the spirit of reform energized the United States.

Progressives wanted to right the wrongs they saw in American life. They pointed their fingers at everything from corrupt government officials to greedy businessmen to shady saloon owners.

Progressives lashed out at railway men who charged outrageous prices to farmers for shipping their crops to market. Progressives also criticized factory owners who expected children to work 10-hour days. Progressive government leaders battled big business, whose monopolies prevented fair trade and kept prices artificially high. Suffragists were progressives, too.

But when Harriot Blatch returned to the United States, she found the women's suffrage movement in a "rut worn deep and ever deeper." The suffrage movement in America had turned downright boring.

Like her gifted mother, Blatch had a flair for choosing just the right words to push her agenda. She also applied new techniques to build publicity for women's suffrage. A "social media" pioneer in the first decade of the 20th century, Blatch decided that suffragists needed to make a splash. It was time for women to move from quiet tea parties at home to the streets of America. She organized rallies and parades, and suffragists sported cheerful purple, green, and white sashes to identify with their cause.

Blatch made sure that the marchers encompassed women from all walks of American life. Many working-class women had joined to push for votes for women. Now suffrage parades boasted women from all rungs on America's social ladder. Once a middle-class venture, the cause now welcomed women from all social classes, from the very rich to the working poor.

In the New York parade of 1911, the plight of working women was on everyone's mind, whether middle class, rich, or poor. The Triangle Shirtwaist Company, a factory where workers sewed clothes, had caught on fire just two months earlier. The workers, mostly young immigrant women, died in the blaze or jumped off the roof and perished. The fire took 146 lives; the last six of the bodies were not identified until a hundred years later.

The Triangle Shirtwaist fire provided deadly evidence that America's working women had the same right to speak their minds as did their "betters." Well-off society women had long felt it was their duty to give money to the poor, but now both groups of women realized that they needed the vote in order to reform society.

At the same time, working women reminded their wealthy associates that working people deserved quality lives as well. One of their leaders, a Russian immigrant named Rose Schneiderman, made a speech with a rich visual image that caught people's imaginations: "What the woman who labors wants is the right to live, not simply exist—the right to life as the rich woman has the right to life, and the sun and music and art.... The worker must have bread, but she must have roses, too."

Rose Schneiderman also believed that she deserved the right to vote.

Despite their best efforts, suffragists ran into the same roadblocks over and over in the early 1900s. As always, the liquor industry used its wealth to influence city officials and members of Congress against woman's suffrage.

States in the "Solid South" created another obstacle. Among their Jim Crow laws were rules that blocked black men from voting. Southern legislators, satisfied with rules that kept white men in power, had no plans to give the vote to white—or black—women. They argued that the states' rights clause in the US Constitution permitted them to set up laws for voting.

★ **Rose Schneiderman, a labor leader, demanded both "bread and roses" for working women.**
Library of Congress mnwp.275025

9

Parades, Pickets, and Prison

ENGLAND'S SUFFRAGISTS called themselves "suffragettes." The suffragettes launched their push for votes later than their American sisters, but when they finally organized they came on loud and strong. Led by Emmeline Pankhurst and her daughters, Christabel and Sylvia, suffragettes believed that their actions would speak louder than their words.

The Pankhursts and their backers used the strategy of civil disobedience. They broke laws—in nonviolent ways—in order to bring attention to the issue of women's suffrage. They chained themselves to fences and called for the British prime minister to act. Suffragettes piled into galleries to catcall at men in session in Parliament, home to Great Britain's House of Commons and House of Lords. They sneaked

★ OPPOSITE: Women and girls, white and black, dressed in white to march for suffrage. Library of Congress LC-USZ62-10845

93

onto a royal golf course and replaced pin flags with their own suffragette ones.

Correctly guessing that this civil disobedience would get them publicity, suffragettes broke laws and landed in prison. Many went on hunger strikes, refusing to eat. In turn, prison officials struck back by forcibly feeding them, a brutal act of shoving a hose down a woman's throat or nose and pouring liquids into her stomach.

Sister Suffragettes

Two YOUNG Americans, both in England during the uproar, became suffragettes, marched with the others, and were arrested. The pair, Alice Paul and Lucy Burns, first met in a British police station where they were jailed. They went on hunger strikes and shared the torture of being forcibly fed.

By the time they were released, Paul and Burns had learned the lessons of British-style protests. Paul sailed home to the United States, ready to shake things up. Burns returned later to serve as Paul's right-hand woman. Both strong willed, Paul and Burns vowed to battle for women's rights in the United States.

Burns was red-haired with a loud voice; Paul was petite and quiet, but her dark eyes glowed with an intensity that was almost scary. Both were well educated. Paul grew up in a Quaker family that took women's equality for granted and sent their daughters to college. Burns's father also believed in educating women, and Burns was a college graduate, too. Neither Paul nor Burns liked the way American suffragists were going about their work. Paul and Burns were a generation younger

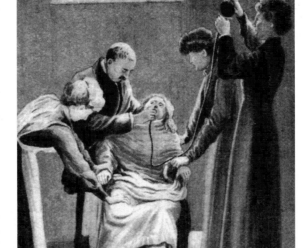

★ LEFT: By the early 1900s, even cereal companies backed the idea of votes for women.

★ BELOW: British suffragettes and American suffragists were forcibly fed in prison. This image of a forcible feeding appeared in July 1912 in *Popular Mechanics* magazine. The Collection of the Public Library of Cincinnati and Hamilton County

than Carrie Catt and Anna Shaw, America's leading suffragists. Catt, Shaw, and their National American Woman Suffrage Association (NAWSA) still held to their long-term strategy: win the vote state by state.

Paul and Burns, however, wanted to win suffrage with one grand act: to amend the US Constitution. Senators and congressmen were the ones standing in their way. To succeed, Paul suggested that the NAWSA suffragists establish a committee to take their cause directly to Congress. As she pointed out, "It is not a war of women against men, for the men are helping loyally, but a war of women and men together against the politicians."

Older suffragists hesitated to approve Paul's request for a congressional committee. Paul and Burns needed support, and they turned to none other than Jane Addams, who was regarded as an American saint. Addams advised the younger women to turn down their volume as they pushed for their ideas. But Addams agreed to back their plan, and NAWSA's leaders accepted Paul's request. Alice Paul's Congressional committee set up shop.

Paul had no plans to stay quiet. In the next few years, she and Burns transformed the small committee into the powerful Congressional Union and moved into a building across the street from the White House. The White House, and the president who lived there,

would become Paul's target in winning the vote.

As Paul, Burns, and their followers became ever stronger, their activist stance became too much to handle for the moderate, well-behaved women at NAWSA. In 1915, the two groups split, and the Congressional Union

★ **ABOVE:** Alice Paul copied the suffragette strategy she learned in Britain. Library of Congress LC-USZ62-37937

★ **RIGHT:** American suffragist Lucy Burns (*left*) admired British suffragette Emmeline Pankhurst (*center*). Library of Congress LC-H261-3299

took its new name, the National Woman's Party (NWP).

Once again, America's suffragists had torn apart, just as they had more than 40 years earlier. On one side stood NAWSA, middle of the road and relatively quiet in its quest for women's suffrage. On the other was Alice Paul, backed up by Lucy Burns and the NWP, who believed in action, not words. They became militants, the rabble-rousers of American suffrage.

★ The cover of the suffrage parade's program was splashed with the National Woman's Party purple and gold.

Library of Congress LC-DIG-ppmsca-12512

Taking a cue from British suffragettes, who worked against the political party in charge in London, Paul decided to go after the political party then in power in Washington, DC—the Democratic Party.

After 15 years of Republican presidents, the Democrats had won the campaign of 1912 and elected Woodrow Wilson as president. Paul's first big effort took place on March 3, 1913, the day that Wilson arrived in Washington to be sworn into office.

When the president-elect's train pulled into the station in the capital, there was no crowd to greet him. "Where are the people?" an aide was heard to ask. "Over … watching the suffrage parade," came the answer.

Paul had upstaged Wilson by holding a parade on the very same day. Eight thousand strong, the parade wound down Pennsylvania Avenue. At the front rode a woman on a white horse. There were floats and bands, foreign delegates, male suffragists, college students, factory women, and representatives from Howard University, a local black college. To keep the parade about suffrage and not about race, these African American women were mingled with the male marchers at the back.

On the steps of the US Treasury Department, women in white staged a tableau, with the figure of Columbia as their leader. Standing silently, these costumed performers portrayed American ideals: liberty, charity, justice, peace, and hope among them.

Half a million people crowded the parade route. Some were there to watch, but others were there to make trouble. Plenty of men despised the thought of women getting the vote. Pushing and shoving and name-calling began, and as the parade wound on, things fell apart and turned ugly.

The *Woman's Journal* reported the following:

Women were spat upon, … [s]lapped in the face, tripped up, pelted with burning cigar stubs, and insulted by jeers and obscene language too

Ida Wells-Barnett

One of the African American women who marched in the Washington suffrage parade did not do as she was told. Ida Wells-Barnett was a member of the Illinois suffrage delegation who traveled to Washington to join in the suffrage parade.

When she arrived, parade organizers told her that she could not march with the rest of the delegation, which was made up of white women. As a black woman, she must march with others like her at the end of the parade. But Wells-Barnett had a different idea. She mingled with the crowd, and when the Illinois women marched past, she walked into the street and joined in. Nothing was going to stop her from marching with Illinois's suffragists.

Wells-Barnett was a member of America's small but well-educated black middle class. Born Ida B. Wells, she made her name by refusing to give up her seat in a whites-only railroad car. She was one of the first American women to join her maiden and married names with a hyphen.

Wells-Barnett was a journalist, and she worked to improve the lives of black women and men in segregated America. Above all, she was known to black Americans for her campaign to stop the horrible practice of lynching.

★ **Ida Wells-Barnett.**
Library of Congress LC-USZ62-107756

In the segregated America of the late 1800s and well into the 1900s, lynching was an act of terror carried out by whites against blacks. White mobs kidnapped and killed black men by lynching—hanging—them. The mobs justified their brutal actions by saying that their black victims had committed terrible crimes.

Wells-Barnett used the power of her pen to bring these cruel acts to America's attention. An ardent suffragist, Wells-Barnett believed winning the vote would fortify her work.

vile to print or repeat.—"Rowdies seized and mauled young girls."—"A very gray-haired college woman was knocked down."—"The parade was continually stopped by the turbulence of the crowd."

The police stood by and did nothing to help. One hundred people went to Emergency Hospital. In the midst of all the confusion, one thing now was clear. The women's suffrage movement was going to cause a fuss.

★ ABOVE: Suffragists staged a tableau at the US Treasury Department steps during their monumental parade in Washington, DC, in 1913. Library of Congress LC-USZ62-70382

★ RIGHT: The *Woman's Journal* printed a headline about the "disgraceful" crowd at the event. Library of Congress LC-DIG-ppmsca-02970

ACTIVITY ▸ Dress Up for Suffrage

SUFFRAGISTS wrote and performed in plays to bring their ideas to large audiences. Often their costumes followed patriotic themes that recalled ancient Greece, the cradle of democracy. Suffragists, like the ancient Greeks, dressed up in white to portray Lady Liberty, Columbia, peace, and justice.

Greek men crowned their heads with laurel leaves when they won sports events. Greek women wore their hair in fanciful styles with twists and braids and often with hair decorations as well. Check out the examples at www.fashion-era.com.

With a few things you have at home or will easily find at a craft store, you can costume yourself like an ancient Greek. Wrap your head in glory!

You'll Need
➤ Adult helper
➤ Marker
➤ Paper
➤ Scissors
➤ Cardboard
➤ Tacky craft glue
➤ Wide plastic headband
➤ Silver spray paint
➤ Old sandals or flip-flops
➤ White T-shirt
➤ White twin sheet
➤ Large safety pins or costume pins

To make your laurel wreath, use the marker to trace the leaf pattern on this page onto a piece of paper and cut it out. Then transfer the leaf pattern to a piece of cardboard and cut the leaves out.

Working on a covered surface, glue the leaves to the headband. Follow the example and overlap them as you work your way around. When you are pleased with the effect, set the wreath aside to dry.

Spray paint the wreath and sandals or flip-flops. Follow the directions on the spray can, and be sure to spray outside in an open area with lots of fresh air.

Are you ready to dress in your costume? Put on the white T-shirt. To make your toga, start by folding a sheet in half lengthwise, as shown. Place one folded corner under your arm and wrap the sheet around you once. Fasten the sheet snugly with a safety pin. Continue to wrap the sheet around you until you have about 4 feet left. Drape this end across your chest and over your shoulder. Use more pins to fasten the sheet to your shirt. Now arrange the folds in your toga.

Slip into your footwear and put your laurel wreath on your head. Who are you? Peace? Columbia? Justice? Liberty? No matter whom you portray, you are standing up for suffrage!

The Antis

Not only men opposed women's suffrage. Plenty of women stood strong against the idea, and they organized committees in Eastern cities, though their efforts did not catch on with women who lived west of Ohio. The Association Opposed to Suffrage for Women, the "Antis," argued that most women did not want the vote and that their place was at home.

Women like Josephine Dodge of New York quietly recruited members at parlor meetings. Always known as "Mrs. Arthur Dodge," she had pioneered day care for working mothers. Dodge worried that winning the vote would lead women into immoral ways.

Carrie Catt was pleased to hear that sometimes these tea parties backfired. At one of these antisuffrage gatherings, a guest became "so indignant at what she heard" she wrote a check for $10,000 for the

★ A pair of campaign buttons shows both sides of the suffrage movement.

suffragists. It was the biggest donation any living person had ever given to win votes for women. (Today that gift would be worth more than $230,000.)

Nationwide efforts to ban alcoholic drinks were as strong as ever. As always, the liquor industry worked against suffrage as well. Catt suspected that the Antis quietly worked with liquor sellers. Suffragists "believed that a trail led from the women's organization into the liquor camp and that it was traveled by the men the women Antis employed."

The Antis did their work state by state, sending a man and a woman to work together. The woman met with other women to gain their support against suffrage. The Anti men met with other men, including liquor dealers and their political buddies.

The well-organized Antis made the front pages of newspapers everywhere. There was plenty of room for disagreement on this burning issue in American life.

VOTES FOR ~~WOMEN~~

We've troubles of our own. Leave well enough alone.

POST CARD

This side for Correspondence.   This side for Address.

★ Did the man who sent this postcard in 1914 agree with its message?

America Goes to War

THE SUFFRAGE movement pained Woodrow Wilson. When he entered the White House, the new president did not take suffragists seriously. Even in the second decade of the new, modern century, most American men still did not think women needed to vote. A young suffragist, Doris Stevens, wrote about a meeting between Wilson and suffragists.

> *Dr. Anna Howard Shaw led the interview. In reply to her eloquent appeal for his assistance, the President said in part: "I am merely the spokesman of my party.... I am not at liberty to urge upon Congress in messages, policies which have not had the ... consideration of those for whom I am spokesman...."*
>
> *[Shaw's] clear, deep, resonant voice ... was in sharp contrast to the halting, timid, little, and technical answer of the President.... Dr. Shaw had dramatically asked, "Mr. President, if you cannot speak for us and your party will not, who then, pray, is there to speak for us?"*
>
> *"You seem very well able to speak for yourselves, ladies," he said with a broad smile.*
>
> *"We mean, Mr. President, who will speak for us with authority?" came back the hot retort from Dr. Shaw.*
>
> *The President made no reply.*

Moderate suffragists like Carrie Catt and Anna Shaw annoyed Woodrow Wilson, and militants like Alice Paul and Lucy Burns outraged him. In January 1917, suffragists appeared on the sidewalk along the iron fence outside the White House. They carried colorful banners and picket signs with messages to the president. The demonstrators broke no law; the Bill of Rights guaranteed them the freedom to assemble.

But suffragists were only one problem the president faced. In the summer of 1914, a terrorist shot and killed an Austrian archduke who was visiting Serbia. The huge Austro-Hungarian Empire declared war on the tiny Balkan nation.

★ President Woodrow Wilson asked Congress to declare war on Germany in April 1917.

Library of Congress LC-USZC4-10297

★ Dr. Anna Howard Shaw was sketched in pencil at a suffrage meeting.

Europe's governments were caught in a complex web of treaties and friendships. War became certain as European nations joined forces with their friends and allies.

On one side were the Central Powers: Germany, Austria-Hungary, and Italy. On the other was the Triple Entente of France, Great Britain, and Russia. Most of Europe's smaller

Jeannette Rankin

When the House of Representatives voted to approve the 19th Amendment during a vote in 1918, one woman stood up to say "Yea." She was Jeannette Rankin, a proud Montana suffragist and America's first congresswoman, elected in 1916. Rankin made her name in her home state by getting permission to address the Montana legislature on the subject of suffrage. A few years later, voters thanked her for her efforts by sending her to Washington.

Raised on a ranch, Rankin spent her life working for the welfare of others, first as a social worker, then as a suffragist, and finally as a peace activist. She was elected to Congress twice as the nation went to war, the first time before World War I, the second time before World War II. "As a woman, I can't go to war," she said, "and I refuse to send anyone else."

As a pacifist, a person who opposes war of any kind, Rankin's views won her few friends in government or back home. Both times, she lost reelection to Congress.

All her life, Rankin pushed for women's rights and peace between nations. "You can no more win a war than win an earthquake," she declared. Rankin also had bitter words for women who approved of war. She called them "worms" who let their sons go off to war "because they're afraid their husbands will lose their jobs in industry if they protest."

Jeannette Rankin never feared speaking her mind. She continued to work for world peace until her death in 1973 at age 92.

★ **America's first congresswoman, Jeannette Rankin, posed on the balcony of the National Woman's Party headquarters.**
Library of Congress mnwp 156007

countries lined up behind one power or the other.

Over the next four years, this Great War, later named World War I, led to the deaths of 8.5 million soldiers and decimated a generation of young men.

The United States held to a neutral stance, but German submarines began a campaign to sink ships on the Atlantic Ocean. Some carried American passengers. Over the months, the German threat appeared to grow ever greater. By early 1917, war seemed inevitable, and the United States declared war on Germany in April. For the president, the suffragists, and the United States, life would never be the same.

By the summer of 1918, more than 1 million US soldiers had sailed to France to fight Germany. "Our boys" was the loving term applied to the young men who came from all 48 states to fight against the evil Kaiser Bill, as the press nicknamed Germany's leader, Kaiser Wilhelm II.

With the men gone to war, America's women stepped in to do their work. "Every muscle, every brain, must be mobilized if the national aim is to be achieved," wrote Harriot Stanton Blatch. She was talking about American women.

With brains and muscles, American women manufactured ammunition, built airplanes and railroad cars, and hauled heavy blocks of ice in horse-drawn wagons to supply their neighbors' iceboxes. Others dressed in the sober gray uniforms of the American Red Cross to deliver telegrams to the families of soldiers who had been injured or killed. Some women went to war in France to serve as nurses in battlefield hospitals or run canteens where soldiers could get a doughnut and a cup of coffee.

★ **Women worked in munitions plants manufacturing rockets during World War I.**
Library of Congress LC-USZ62-53195

Make a Coat-Hanger Banner

OLD photos of suffragists show them marching with large wire banners that looked somewhat like kites. What's on your mind? Design a banner to broadcast your ideas. It's easy using a coat hanger and some cloth.

You'll Need

- Adult helper
- Wire coat hanger
- Old sheet or piece of light-colored cloth
- Scissors
- Ruler
- Pencil
- Newspaper
- Marker
- Fringe (measuring a bit longer than the hanger, purchased at a fabric store)
- Tacky craft glue

Measure the width of the hanger. Using this measurement, trace a large rectangle on the cloth by following the diagram below. Carefully cut out your rectangle and place your banner vertically so that the long sides run up and down.

Leave a 2-inch margin at the top. Use the ruler to trace light lines for your words. Then lightly write your message in pencil. You can write "Votes for Women" or think of another slogan to voice your thoughts.

Cover a large surface with newspaper. Place your banner over the newspaper.

Use the marker to trace each word. Work neatly and carefully.

Line up the fringe along the bottom of your banner. Trim off any extra. Apply glue along the back edge of the fringe. Place it along the bottom edge of the banner and lightly tap in place with your fingers. Let dry.

Now mount your banner on the hanger. Turn the banner upside down. Fold 1 inch of the top to the back and press it with your fingers. Open it back up and apply a thin strip of glue along the folded-back edge. Place the hanger along the fold. Now seal the edge with your fingers so that the glue holds securely. Let dry.

Fly your banner proudly. If you would like to make another patriotic banner, cut strips of red, white, and blue cloth. Assemble it in the same way. Instead of fringing it, tie the colored strips together in a loose knot.

★ On January 10, 1917, suffragists gathered in front of the National Woman's Party headquarters and prepared to picket—for the first time—in front of the White House.

Library of Congress mnwp.160026

Suffragists remembered the lessons learned long ago during the Civil War. The NAWSA women agreed to do war work, but this time they kept up their push for suffrage too. They did not let the terrible news coming from the battlefields of France silence them.

In people's eyes, this Great War became the "war to save the world for democracy." To Alice Paul and the National Woman's Party, the war became a perfect example of what was wrong in American society. How could American soldiers die in a war for freedom when American women had no freedom to vote?

Alice Paul adjusted her tactics. The messages to President Wilson and the rest of the nation were about to change.

Forcibly Fed

THE NWP grew bolder and louder. In January 1917, protesters carrying picket signs became a regular sight at the White House. In June, the police arrested a few marchers on charges of blocking the sidewalk. As 1917 dragged on, the protests grew more heated. When picketers showed up at the fence outside the White House, their signs screamed with passion. "Mr. President," one read, "how long will women wait for liberty?" Another went further. Harsh words drawn from a Bible passage

ripped the president, comparing him to Germany's leader. "Kaiser Wilson . . . 20,000,000 American women are not self-governed. Take the beam out of your own eye."

Summer melted into fall, and still suffragists showed up outside the White House as the scene got hotter and more women were arrested. By now, judges had sentenced 97 of the women to prison.

Alice Paul was arrested on October 20 and was sentenced with other protesters to jail. Their jailers treated them with contempt. The jail windows stayed locked until the angry women broke one to get some fresh air. At mealtime, the women tried to choke down disgusting meals of raw salt pork, bread, and molasses.

Still, they tried to rebel. Alice Paul and Rose Winslow, a factory worker, declared themselves to be political prisoners, ones who had been thrown in jail because they had protested a law. Their claim surprised and annoyed their jailers—political prisoners didn't show up in American jails.

Weak from not eating, Paul and Winslow were carried into a prison hospital. Together they decided to take drastic action. On November 5, they went on a hunger strike and refused to eat at all. Prison doctors did all they could to prove that Paul was a mental patient. They locked her away in the room, boarded

★ A woman displayed a picket sign outside the White House in 1917. The sign referred to the president as "Kaiser Wilson." Library of Congress mnwp 160030

up one of its windows, and allowed no one, including lawyers, to see her.

Paul insisted that she was a political prisoner and nothing more. Then the forcible feeding began. Winslow and Paul underwent the torture three times a day. Rose Winslow wrote notes on tiny pieces of paper that were smuggled outside.

Alice Paul is in the psychopathic ward. She dreaded forcible feeding frightfully, and I hate to think how she must be feeling. I had a nervous time of it, gasping a long time afterward, and my stomach rejecting during the process. . . . The poor soul who fed me got liberally besprinkled [sprayed with vomit] during the process. I heard myself making the most hideous sounds. . . . One feels so forsaken when [one] lies prone and people shove a pipe down one's stomach.

A Night of Terror

As Paul, Winslow, and others fought their battles in the Washington jail, 41 more women showed up outside the White House to protest with gold-lettered banners and flags in the NWP's colors—purple, white, and gold. Several times they were arrested and released, until finally a judge sentenced them to prison as well. But this time the women were taken to Virginia to a notorious workhouse. They were not prepared for what happened when they arrived at the prison on November 14, 1917.

★ **Barely able to walk, suffragist Dora Lewis was released from prison after living through a "Night of Terror."** Library of Congress mnwp 160039

The jail's superintendent, backed by a group of guards who had not dressed in their uniforms, seized the women and dragged them to their cells. Lucy Burns, her arms manacled to a bar high above her head, hung there all night, barely able to stand. Dorothy Day, later a well-known Catholic social activist, was thrown down twice over the arm of an iron bench. The "elderly Mrs. Lawrence [Dora] Lewis... was literally thrown in. Her head struck the iron bed. We thought she was dead," Doris Stevens, also a prisoner, recalled. Another woman had a heart attack, but the guards paid no attention.

The suffragists followed Alice Paul's example. They declared themselves political prisoners and went on a hunger strike. Lucy Burns and Dora Lewis were forcibly fed. Finally, a sympathetic marine who had seen the violence reported the news to Washington. It took days, but friends of the women went to court to win their freedom.

The jailers stalled. They didn't want anyone to view the prisoners until the women had recovered. When they did appear at court, the women, "haggard, red-eyed, sick," limped to their seats. Others were so weak that they had to be stretched out on the wooden benches in the courtroom. Some "bore the marks of the attack."

The judge ordered the women to be moved back to the Washington jail. There they kept up their hunger strike. They would not give up. Then suddenly, they were released on November 28.

When Americans read the news of suffragists suffering the Night of Terror and forcible feedings, they felt sick, too. The jailers' harsh treatment transformed the suffragists into heroes. Powerful senators and congressmen launched investigations about the brutal attacks. At long last, the issue of votes for women was on the front pages of newspapers everywhere, and Americans could no longer look the other way.

Neither could President Wilson, who found it a relief to deal with the calm, much older Carrie Catt and NAWSA. Members of NAWSA had made no official comments about Alice Paul and her crew. Yet it was plain that the militant suffragists had hit their mark.

Wilson, who respected Catt as much he disrespected Paul, decided to support a constitutional amendment to give women the vote. The weary president needed both women and men to back him as he led the United States during wartime.

On January 10, 1918, Congress met to vote on the 19th Amendment to the Constitution. No one could be sure that the amendment would pass in the US House of Representatives. Every vote counted, and

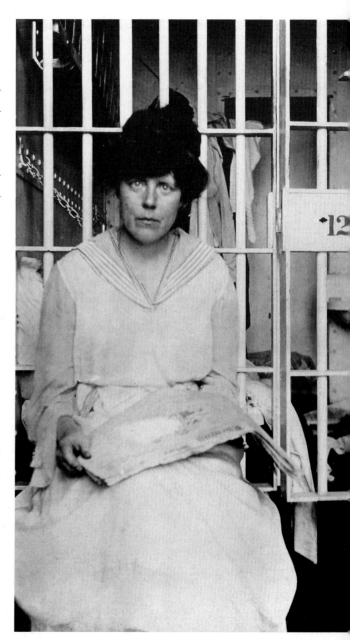

★ **Lucy Burns, dressed in prison garb, sat outside her cell.** Library of Congress mnwp 274009

several representatives turned out in support of women's suffrage.

One congressman, his face showing pain from a broken shoulder, arrived to vote yes. Two others left their hospital beds to do the same. As suffragists watched and waited, Congressman Frederick Hicks arrived from New York. His wife was dying, but he knew she wanted him to vote yes.

There were 410 members in the House of Representatives. A two-to-one majority was needed, and as the congressmen voiced their yeses and nos, the suffragists kept count. When they heard the 274th yes, they rejoiced. In the halls of Congress, happy women sang the old hymn "Praise God from Whom All Blessings Flow."

The congressman from New York went home to bury his wife.

A Senate That Would Not Budge

IN NOVEMBER 1918, World War I came to an end, and Americans celebrated their victory against Germany. The women of Great Britain, Canada, and Germany, too, were given the right to vote. But with the vote for the 19th Amendment held up in the US Senate, militant suffragists kept up their protests.

It took months to persuade a handful of Senate holdouts that women deserved the vote. The suffragists appealed to the president to act. Again they demonstrated, were arrested and jailed, and went on hunger strikes.

In February 1919, yet another band of marchers burned a small picture of President Wilson outside the White House and were sent to prison. Paul won even more publicity by sending the Prison Special, a train loaded with suffragist prisoners, on a cross-country tour. Among them was Louisine Havemeyer, well into her 60s, who had managed to get herself arrested.

As the train steamed from state to state, curious Americans gathered at the stations to hear what the former prisoners had to say. Not all approved of Alice Paul's tactics, but many admired these women who had gone to jail for their beliefs.

By now, both the Republican and Democratic parties backed suffrage. On May 19, 1919, President Wilson called a special session of Congress. Again, the US House of Representatives voted to pass the 19th Amendment. On June 4, it went to the US Senate. Four Southern senators tried to stop the amendment. They felt sure that giving votes to women would make it easier for African Americans to demand their own voting rights in the segregated South.

Louisine Havemeyer

Before she became a suffragist, Louisine Elder Havemeyer had already made her name in America's art world. As a young girl in the 1870s, she lived in Paris with her mother and sister, where she met Mary Cassatt, who was to become the century's most famous woman painter. Over the years, Cassatt introduced Havemeyer to French painters like Edgar Degas and Claude Monet, whose modern works had shaken up Paris's stodgy art world.

Louisine Elder married O. H. "Harry" Havemeyer, a New Yorker who made a fortune in the sugar industry. Havemeyer, an eager collector of art from Japan and China, enthusiastically backed his wife's own art collecting. Over the years, they gathered a huge collection of paintings and sculpture worth millions of dollars. (Today much of their collection appears in New York's Metropolitan Museum of Art.)

Havemeyer learned to support women's rights while she was grow-ing up. Susan Anthony, Lucretia Mott, and Elizabeth Stanton were household names. When she married, Louisine Havemeyer also had her husband's blessing to speak out as well as expand her mind.

After Harry Havemeyer died in 1907, Havemeyer devoted her energy to women's suffrage. She wrote about her experiences for *Scribner's Magazine.* Havemeyer

★ **Louisine Havemeyer, once jailed for protesting at the White House, posed with a policeman during her train tour on the Prison Special.** Library of Congress mnwp 160058

was not afraid to criticize President Wilson, "to whom the thought of mobilized womanpower was as a red rag to an infuriated bull." Her article, "Memories of a Militant" (a very rich, influential militant), made readers think.

When she went to jail, members of Havemeyer's family telegraphed angry messages to her. The family matriarch had let them down. When she visited her daughter's home, her son-in-law refused to welcome her, and she had to sit in the car.

Havemeyer traveled on the Prison Special for 29 days, shaking hands, raising money, and claiming votes for women across America. When the train pulled into the station in New York, she happily noted that the suffragists had won many friends and good publicity. With the typewriters "still clicking and the coins still chinking," she left the train in a hurry to make one more speech—at New York's famed Carnegie Hall.

Sixty-sixth Congress of the United States of America;

At the First Session,

Begun and held at the City of Washington on Monday, the nineteenth day of May,
one thousand nine hundred and nineteen.

JOINT RESOLUTION

Proposing an amendment to the Constitution extending the right of suffrage
to women.

---

*Resolved by the Senate and House of Representatives of the United States
of America in Congress assembled (two-thirds of each House concurring therein),*
That the following article is proposed as an amendment to the Constitution,
which shall be valid to all intents and purposes as part of the Constitution when
ratified by the legislatures of three-fourths of the several States.

" ARTICLE ————.

" The right of citizens of the United States to vote shall not be denied or
abridged by the United States or by any State on account of sex.

" Congress shall have power to enforce this article by appropriate
legislation."

F. H. Gillett

Speaker of the House of Representatives.

Thos. R. Marshall

*Vice President of the United States and
President of the Senate.*

Nonetheless, 66 senators voted "aye." President Wilson was in France at a peace conference. With a gold pen, vice president Thomas Marshall signed the 19th Amendment.

At long last, the men who held power in the nation's capital had done the right thing. The 19th Amendment was on its way to the states. Three-fourths of the 48 state legislatures had to ratify—vote to approve—the 19th Amendment. For suffragists, there was much more to accomplish.

★ **The 19th Amendment.** National Archives

10

Over the Top

I N THE summer of 1920, a Tennessee mother wrote a letter to her 24-year-old son, whose name was Harry Burn. At age 24, he was the youngest member of the all-male Tennessee House of Representatives. Mrs. Febb Burn had followed the newspapers all summer. Sprinkled in with all the news from home were her feelings about votes for women and a reminder:

> *Dear Son...*
>
> *Hurrah and vote for Suffrage and don't keep them in doubt.... I noticed Chandler's [a Tennessee man's] speech. It was very bitter I've been watching to see how you stood, but have not seen anything yet....*
>
> *Don't forget to be a good boy and help Mrs. "Thomas Catt" with her "Rats." Is she the one that put rat in ratification... Ha!...*
>
> *With lots of love*
>
> *Mama*

★ **By 1915, all of the Western states except New Mexico had granted women the right to vote in state and local elections.** Library of Congress LC-USZC2-1206

Taking It to Tennessee

THERE WERE 48 states in the United States of America, so the magic number for women's suffrage was 36. Thirty-six state legislatures had to vote yes on the 19th Amendment. Only then would it become a part of the US Constitution. Only then would American women everywhere have the right to vote.

Suffragists rolled up their sleeves and resumed their campaigning. They were leaving nothing to chance. From the headquarters of both NAWSA and the NWP, suffragists fanned out across the country.

At first, the yeses came quickly. In one month, 11 state legislatures voted for ratification. Within six months, another 11 came onboard. State by state, legislators voiced their approval for women's suffrage. Washington was the 35th state to ratify the amendment.

The summer of 1920 unfolded. Suffragists studied the numbers and considered the rumors that poured in from states that had not voted. The situation in Tennessee looked hopeful. A

★ LEFT: **Page six of Febb Burn's letter to her son Harry.** Harry T. Burn Papers, McClung Historical Collection

★ BELOW: **When Harry Burn opened this envelope, he discovered his mother's views on votes for women.**
Harry T. Burn Papers, McClung Historical Collection

★ RIGHT: **Febb Burn.**
Harry T. Burn Papers, McClung Historical Collection

"yes" from both houses of the Tennessee legislature would push ratification over the top.

Carrie Catt packed her bags and took the train to Nashville, expecting to stay a few days to pitch in and help win votes. As things turned out, she spent over a month in the Tennessee heat and humidity.

At the NWP building in Washington, Alice Paul was stitching a banner. Every time a state voted to ratify the 19th Amendment, she cut out a star and stitched it to the long piece of cloth. By August 15, 1920, Paul had cut and stitched 35 stars onto the banner. She set her needle and thread aside, waiting like everyone else for the Tennessee legislature to change American history forever.

Ratification in Tennessee moved as slowly as the sun on those long summer days. Anti-suffragists poured into the state from all over the country, hoping to make their last stand and to block votes for women. Legislators, suffragists, and Antis packed into the Hermitage Hotel in Nashville. It became a "war of the roses." Suffragists and their male backers wore yellow roses, and the Antis sported red ones.

Mysterious men showed up to work quietly behind the scenes. They paid bribes to any Tennessee legislators willing to take money and vote no on suffrage. Upstairs in rooms at the Hermitage Hotel, liquor dealers held

parties for the legislators, hoping to win their votes against suffrage. Tennessee bourbon and moonshine whiskey—both outlawed—flowed into their guests' glasses.

All around, the dirty dogs of politics showed their teeth. A notable representative who had pledged his support for suffrage changed his mind. Then, without warning, more legislators backed off.

The suffragists did not have to worry about the Tennessee Senate, which quickly voted its approval by an overwhelming vote of 25 to 4. Then it came time for the Tennessee House to vote. There were 96 representatives. Forty-nine votes were needed for ratification to pass. Suffragists waited nervously.

When Harry Burn stood up to voice his vote on ratification, he wore the red rose of the Antis pinned to his lapel. The men in his district didn't support votes for women. But in his pocket was the letter from his mother. Burn had taken her words to heart. He voted "aye."

Harry Burn's vote put the "rat" in ratification of the 19th Amendment, giving women the right the vote throughout the United States of America. In the exact words that Susan B. Anthony had written in 1878, the 19th Amendment became the law of the land: "The right of citizens of the United States to vote shall not be denied or abridged by the United States or by any State on account of sex."

★ **Harry Burn's vote made women's suffrage the law of the land.** Harry T. Burn Papers, McClung Historical Collection

Make a Five-Pointed Star with Just One Cut

ACCORDING to legend, George Washington and two other Revolutionary leaders asked Betsy Ross to stitch the first American flag with five-pointed stars. She folded up a piece of paper and, with just one snip of her scissors, cut a perfect star.

We don't know whether Alice Paul used the same technique when she cut out the stars for her suffrage banner. However, you can create five-pointed stars with one cut, just like Betsy Ross did.

You'll Need
➤ White paper
➤ Scissors
➤ Ruler
➤ Pencil

First practice using paper to cut five-pointed stars. Trim a piece of paper into a square by matching the top edge to one side and trimming away the excess with scissors.

Measure halfway down the length of the fold and mark that spot with the pencil. Now measure 2¼ inches down from the upper

right-hand corner of the paper and place a mark there as well. Draw a line to join both marks and fold along the line.

Place the paper facing you as shown. Fold along the dotted line, bringing the bottom point up and over as shown.

Place the paper on your work surface as shown. You now have a "kite" shape facing you.

It's time for one last fold. Bring the two edges together and fold as shown.

Do you see the triangle? Measure and mark a point 3 inches from the upper left-hand point. Now draw a line from the mark to the opposite corner.

Now it's time to make just *one* cut along the line. Pick up your scissors and cut!

Pull the extra bits of paper away and unfold your star. How do you think Betsy Ross learned to cut a star this way? (There are easier methods used in origami, which is the Japanese art of paper folding. You can look them up on the Internet.)

Now that you can cut out such cool stars, how can you use them? Look around the house for other kinds of paper to fold and cut your creations.

On Election Day in November 1920, women took their place in line along with men at polls across the nation to vote for a new president. However, one elderly woman long past her 90th birthday was too sick to get to her polling place. She was Charlotte Woodward Pierce, the frustrated glove maker who had gone with her friends to the Seneca Falls women's rights convention in 1848. Pierce was the only person at the meeting who lived long enough to see women win the vote. In the end, she died before she could ever cast a ballot.

The End of the Beginning

SURE THAT their work was complete, the National American Woman Suffrage Association disbanded. Carrie Chapman Catt went on to serve as the first president of the League of Women Voters.

Alice Paul added the final star to her banner, but she believed that a woman's work was never done. Women had the vote, and now there was more to accomplish. Always the realist, Paul saw that women lacked true economic power.

The history of the 1900s proved that she was correct. For most of the century, women were

★ **Charlotte Woodward Pierce waited all her life for the right to vote.** Library of Congress LC-F81-11964

paid less than men for working the same jobs. Most top jobs stayed closed to them. Women were welcome to work as secretaries or clerks, but they seldom sat in the boss's corner office.

In trade jobs where men worked with their hands, women weren't welcome either. Except when men went overseas to fight during World War II, women could not hold jobs

★ Alice Paul unfurled her banner to celebrate the hard-won battle for women's suffrage.

Library of Congress mnwp 160068

You Be the Judge

CARTOONS often are filled with powerful symbols. The cartoon below about women's suffrage appeared in 1918. The artist who drew it hoped to get a reaction from his readers.

What's your reaction? Study the cartoon carefully. What do you think the cartoonist thought about suffragists? Did he support or oppose votes for women?

To help you judge the cartoon, think about what images the artist chose. How did he draw them? Where did he place them? What do the stair steps symbolize? How do the words he chose have meaning?

Most important, how do you feel when you look at this cartoon? Are you amused? Confused? Annoyed? What kinds of emotions rise in you? Are you surprised at your reaction?

WOMAN SUFFRAGE
1920-1970
RIGHT TO VOTE
VOTES FOR WOMEN
U.S. 6¢
50ᵀᴴ ANNIVERSARY

★ A postage stamp celebrated the 50th anniversary of women's suffrage in 1970.

United States Post Office

★ Library of Congress LC-DIG-ppmsca-02940

building cars on assembly lines or work as plumbers, welders, electricians, or mechanics.

When Americans began to travel more frequently on airplanes in the 1960s, women served as flight attendants (then called "stewardesses"), but only men could hold the high-status job of pilot. Some women worked as lawyers, doctors, engineers, or scientists. A handful became astronauts. Not until the end of the 20th century did women begin to rise to top jobs in companies. To do so, businesswomen felt they had to break through an invisible "glass ceiling" of discrimination.

Some women served in Congress, but women didn't begin to achieve true political power until late in the 1900s. In 1984, Geraldine Ferraro was nominated to run for vice president of the United States as a Democrat, and in 2008, the Republican Party also nominated a woman—Sarah Palin—as their candidate for vice president.

During that long presidential campaign of 2008, it appeared that a woman, Hillary Rodham Clinton, would win the Democratic Party nomination to run for president of the United States. However, she was defeated in primary elections by a male African American senator, Barack Obama, who surprised the nation by declaring his candidacy. He went on to become the nation's first president of color.

Most Americans have forgotten the story of women's struggle to win the vote. But Alice Paul never forgot, and she always looked forward to improve women's lives. In 1923, Paul wrote an Equal Rights Amendment to the Constitution. It said, "Equality of rights under the law shall not be denied or abridged by the United States or by any state on account of sex."

Paul believed that this amendment would give women the economic power they deserved in America's workplaces. It took until 1972 for the amendment to pass through Congress. This "ERA" was sent to the states for ratification, but it had a deadline. As with the suffrage movement 100 years earlier, the ERA divided Americans. Only 35 state legislatures voted yes, and the amendment withered away after 1982. Paul died in 1977, never to see her amendment ratified.

Equal rights for women are not yet the law of the land in the United States.

★ A Tennessee cartoonist understood the history behind the 19th Amendment when he drew this image. Tennessee Historical Society

Resources

EXPLORE THE history of women's suffrage with books, music, and websites. One of the best ways to start is to visit a library and ask a librarian to help you.

Books to Read

Bausum, Ann. *With Courage and Cloth: Winning the Fight for a Woman's Right to Vote*. Washington, DC: National Geographic, 2004.

Burns, Ken, Martha Saxton, Ann D. Gordon, Ellen Carol Dubois, Paul Barnes, and Geoffrey C. Ward. *Not for Ourselves Alone: The Story of Elizabeth Cady Stanton and Susan B. Anthony*. New York: Knopf, 1999.

Colman, Penny. *Elizabeth Cady Stanton and Susan B. Anthony: A Friendship That Changed the World*. New York: Henry Holt, 2011.

Dumbeck, Kristina. *Leaders of Women's Suffrage*. San Diego: Lucent Books, 2000.

Fradin, Dennis Brindell, and Judith Bloom Fradin. *Ida B. Wells: Mother of the Civil Rights Movement*. New York: Clarion, 2000.

Helmer, Diana Starr. *Women Suffragists*. New York: Facts on File, 1998.

Macdonald, Fiona. *You Wouldn't Want to Be a Suffragist*. New York: Franklin Watts, 2008.

Macy, Sue. *Wheels of Change*. Washington, DC: National Geographic Children's Books, 2011.

Stanton, Elizabeth Cady. *Eighty Years and More: Reminiscences 1815–1897*. (Many editions of Stanton's highly readable memoirs are available as print or electronic publications.)

Places to Visit in Person or Online

Frances Willard House Museum

1730 Chicago Avenue
Evanston, IL 60201
(847) 328-7500
www.franceswillardhouse.org

The Frances Willard House Museum, a National Historic Landmark, showcases furniture, artwork, textiles, family photographs, books, and Willard's bicycle—all of which help tell the story of this famous social reformer.

Harriet Beecher Stowe Center

77 Forest Street
Hartford, CT 06105
(860) 522-9258
www.harrietbeecherstowecenter.org

The Harriet Beecher Stowe Center uses Stowe's life and work to inspire visitors to change their world. A guided tour of the Stowe House provides an intimate glimpse into the life of the author who wrote the groundbreaking antislavery novel *Uncle Tom's Cabin*.

Lowell National Historical Park

304 Dutton Street
Lowell, MA 01852
(978) 970-5000
www.nps.gov/lowe

Lowell National Historical Park preserves and interprets the history of the American Industrial Revolution in Lowell, Massachusetts. The park in downtown Lowell includes historic cotton textile mills, 5.6 miles of power canals, operating gatehouses, and worker housing. Its Mill Girls & Immigrants Exhibit explores the history of "mill girls" and immigrants in a Boott Mills boardinghouse.

Matilda Joslyn Gage Home

210 East Genesee Street
Fayetteville, NY 13066
(315) 637-9511
www.maltildajoslyngage.org

The Matilda Joslyn Gage Foundation offers tours of the Gage home in Fayetteville, New York. Gage was a close collaborator with Susan B. Anthony and Elizabeth Cady Stanton in the suffrage movement. The Family Parlor and Oz Room hold special interest for young visitors; here Gage spent hours talking with her son-in-law L. Frank Baum, the author of *The Wizard of Oz*—he was dedicated to social reform.

National Women's Hall of Fame

76 Fall Street
PO Box 335
Seneca Falls, NY 13148
(315) 568-8060
www.greatwomen.org

The National Women's Hall of Fame is the nation's oldest membership organization honoring the achievements of distinguished American women.

Seneca Falls Historical Society Museum

55 Cayuga Street
Seneca Falls, NY 13148
(315) 568-8412
www.sfhistoricalsociety.org

The Seneca Falls Historical Society Museum is housed in a late Victorian-era residence and showcases how a large Victorian family lived in the later 1800s.

Susan B. Anthony Museum & House

17 Madison Street
Rochester, NY 14608
(585) 235-6124
www.susanbanthonyhouse.org

The Susan B. Anthony Museum & House keeps her vision alive by preserving and sharing Anthony's National Historic Landmark home and offers these resources through tours, publications, its website, and interpretive programs.

The Women's Museum:
An Institute for the Future

3800 Parry Avenue
Dallas, TX 75226
(214) 915-0860
www.thewomensmuseum.org

The Women's Museum: An Institute for the Future is associated with the Smithsonian Institution. Located in Fair Park in Dallas, Texas, the Women's Museum's 70,000-square-foot space houses programs and exhibits where visitors can honor the past and explore the contributions of women in history.

Women's Rights National Historical Park

136 Fall Street
Seneca Falls, NY 13148
Visitor Information: (315) 568-0024
Park Headquarters: (315) 568-2991
www.nps.gov/wori

The Women's Rights National Park in Seneca Falls, New York, has a visitor's center and four sites that played a role in the early suffrage movement, including Elizabeth Cady Stanton's home and Wesleyan Chapel, the site of the first women's rights convention.

Internet Sites

Charlotte Woodward Pierce

www.nps.gov/wori/historyculture/charlotte
  -woodward.htm
Visit this site to read more about Charlotte Woodward Pierce.

The Elizabeth Cady Stanton & Susan B. Anthony Papers Project

http://ecssba.rutgers.edu/index.html

This Rutgers University project directs older readers toward more resources about these two leaders in women's suffrage.

Lucy Stone

www.teachushistory.org/second-great
  -awakening-age-reform/resources
  /lucy-stone-film

A short film about Lucy Stone appears on this website.

National Women's History Project

http://nwhp.org
The National Women's History Project recognizes and celebrates the diverse historical accomplishments of women. Although its website is geared toward adults, the NWHP offers valuable information about how it is "writing women back into history."

Index

Page numbers in *italics* refer to pages with images.